BLOOMING PAPER

how to handcraft paper flowers and botanicals

LAURA REED

SCHIFFER PUBLISHING

4880 Lower Valley Road • Atglen, PA 19310

DEDICATION AND THANKS

For Ada and Stanley, but mostly for Mike, who encouraged and enabled me throughout x

Thanks to GF Smith for all of the beautiful paper, HobbyCraft for the amazing materials
and tools, and Cricut for the brilliant digital cutting machine

Other Schiffer Books on Related Subjects:

*Paper Joy for Every Room: 15 Fun Projects to Add Decorating
Charm to Your Home*, Laure Farion, ISBN 978-0-7643-6055-8

Library of Congress Control Number: 2020952532

Produced by BlueRed Press Ltd. 2021
Designed by Matt Windsor
Type set in Avenir

ISBN: 978-0-7643-6208-8
Printed in India

Published by Schiffer Publishing, Ltd.
4880 Lower Valley Road
Atglen, PA 19310
Phone: (610) 593-1777; Fax: (610) 593-2002
Email: Info@schifferbooks.com
Web: www.schifferbooks.com

For our complete selection of fine books on this and related
subjects, please visit our website at www.schifferbooks.com.
You may also write for a free catalog.

Schiffer Publishing's titles are available at special discounts
for bulk purchases for sales promotions or premiums. Special
editions, including personalized covers, corporate imprints, and
excerpts, can be created in large quantities for special needs.
For more information, contact the publisher.

We are always looking for people to write books on new and
related subjects. If you have an idea for a book, please contact
us at proposals@schifferbooks.com.

CONTENTS

INTRODUCTION

ABOUT THE AUTHOR

When it comes to making and craft, I would describe myself as a jack-of-all-trades. In childhood my sisters and I were encouraged to create: I learned to knit, sew, cut, glue, and build. At school, I was very interested in painting, then I progressed to an Art and Design foundation course. The purpose of this year was to experiment with different disciplines and find "the one" to study at degree level. I was in my element and surprised even myself when, in the end, I chose to specialize in 3-D design.

After designing and making a range of diverse items from knitted handbags to a dining table, I graduated with a degree in furniture and product design. Despite using paper and card a lot for model making and experimentation at university, paper crafting didn't fully present itself to me for another six years.

Instead I worked in retail display design, starting as a mannequin dresser and progressing my way up to a senior designer at an agency, which designed for top-end and main street brands. My last job before becoming full time self-employed was in-house at the head office of a big main street brand. Then, when I got engaged, "project wedding" became the perfect opportunity for me to combine my education, hobbies, and commercial production experience.

We made a conscious decision not to spend a lot of money on our big day, so to help with that goal, I made and crafted everything that I possibly could for fun. Among other things, I made hundreds of paper flowers for the tables. Our wedding was featured online, and after its publication I started to receive orders from other couples, and requests from stylists and planners to make props for photo shoots.

Paper flowers emerged as my specialty quite early on, and I have improved and honed my skills ever since. I have made paper flowers for countless weddings: bouquets, buttonholes, reception decorations, anything that requires embellishment. The largest flower I have made (as I write this), is a 3.3 ft. (1 m) wide, double-sided, paper rose for a window display in London.

When I started out, my flowers were quite simple. The more I practiced, the more elaborate they became. I like to make graphic, stylized pieces, but when my sister challenged me to make some more realistic flowers for her bridal bouquet, my range expanded even further.

Natural flowers inspire my designs along with graphic and textile design. (I go into more depth on the design process in the "Designs to Inspire" chapter.) My evolution of paper flower making has been quite organic over the years; the starting point and process are mirrored in this book.

When I started to teach paper flower craft workshops, the idea for this book really began to develop. There is something so simple and accessible about paper, and how easily it can be made into a 3-D form by using only scissors and glue. Rewardingly, workshop attendees respond really positively to the process.

It's so easy to get lost in making paper flowers, whether you are a beginner or an experienced crafter—in today's fraught world, that can only be a good thing! I have been asked countless numbers of times whether I have written a book about the process—with this volume, I have! And it seems a perfect opportunity to bring this wonderful craft to a wider audience.

ABOUT THE BOOK

This book is aimed at beginners as well as people who have some paper crafting experience, so I will go through the basic techniques of paper flower making, and the process of designing paper blooms. There will be lots of opportunity to practice, as I believe you can learn this craft best through experimenting and trying different techniques, to find what works best for you.

My mantra is "It's not wrong, it's different." You really can't do this craft incorrectly: so-called mistakes just lead to alternative effects or finished flowers, teaching new techniques and methods along the way.

Once we have gone over the basics and I have told you about my favorite tools and materials, there are step-by-step instructions for both individual flowers and full floral projects. The final chapter shows you the process behind my larger-scale paper flower installations, and right at the back, you'll find all of the templates you need, labeled and sorted by chapter or project.

There are three ways you can use this book:
1—follow the chapters from start to finish, learning techniques, practicing individual flowers, and then moving on to the designed projects;
2—use the flowers from the practice chapters to make your own floral pieces;
3—use the techniques to design your own unique blooms and projects.

If you are a complete beginner, I recommend starting from the beginning of the book and working your way through. However, if you really want to try one project in particular, you can jump right in and refer back to the relevant flower instructions.

Whichever way you decide to use this book, you will pick up new methods and ways of doing things as you go. My aim is for you to develop your own techniques and approaches as you experiment and practice. But above all, have some fun, and a little mindful time-out.

Just remember, "It's not wrong, it's different!"

ABOUT THE TEMPLATES

At the back of this book, you will find all of the templates that you need to make the flowers and projects in the guided chapters, apart from some of the pieces for the Garland project. These are upsized versions of other flowers, and the scaling dimensions are given at the beginning of the Garland entry. You could also try experimenting with the scale on any one of the other flowers in this book.

Either trace the templates directly from the page and then transfer them to your chosen media (you could also make thicker card templates for reuse from the shapes), or scan/photograph the pages and print the shapes directly onto your paper of choice. If you're using a digital cutting machine, scan in and trace the shapes in the software for that machine.

You can also find all of the templates (including for all of the Garland components) at full size on the publisher's website at *www.schifferbooks.com/bloomingpapertemplates*

MATERIALS

One of the biggest draws to this craft is the results that can be achieved with the humblest of materials and simplest of tools. You don't need anything specialized and are very likely to have the basics at home already. However, if you catch the blooming paper bug, there are lots of extra bits of kit you can invest in!

N.B. Numbers in parenthesis on pages 8–11 relate to the photograph above.

PAPER AND CARD (1)

I prefer to use card stock and paper (rather than crepe or tissue paper) as it gives nice, crisp, graphic quality to the finished flowers. It is surprisingly adaptable, and you can make both stylized and realistic flowers, as well as complementary foliage.

I use a mix of weights, textures, and finishes in my projects as they each give slightly varied effects, reflect light differently, and add interest to the finished piece. Once you have practiced some flowers, you may well get a feel for which papers you like working with best. It's fun to try crafting with repurposed paper too. For my own wedding, I made paper flowers out of maps, music scores, and even the pages from an old technical car manual, which had lots of engineering diagrams.

The most important thing here is to experiment, and use a color or texture you love! One of the best things about teaching paper flower workshops is seeing how different each person's flowers are by the end, despite everyone starting off by learning the same processes and techniques and using much the same materials.

Color

When choosing paper or card, color is the main factor for me. I like to think of where the finished display will live, or whom I am crafting for. Couples getting married tend to have very specific color schemes in mind. But, if I am creating a window display (see page 138 for an example), I will consider the retailer's branding and the interior of the store.

For some projects, like the Bouquet (see page 124), a neutral palette, inspired by nature, works well. Equally, a bright color scheme, like the one used for the Chandelier (see page 113), can be really fun and effective.

I have suggested colors for each step-by-step project in this book, but please do adapt them to your taste and the paper available to you.

Weight/gsm

The abbreviation "gsm" stands for grams per square meter. No matter what size of sheet you use, its gsm will be determined by the equivalent weight of a piece that is 1 meter (39.37 in.) square.

In general, I would start practicing using something between 80 gsm (standard printer paper) and around 130 gsm (thin card / thick paper). Try different weights; experimenting is the best way to find out what you like to work with.

Don't get bogged down with gsm weights unless you want to make a really huge flower (in which case, thicker is better) or something super tiny (where you will make life easier for yourself if you choose something more lightweight).

Sometimes, US weights are given in pounds (lbs.). Printing paper (75–90 gsm) is the equivalent of 50–60 lb. text. Thin card of 135–145 gsm could either be 36–40 lb. bond or around 67 lb. Bristol. If in doubt, ask your supplier.

Size

All projects are based on A4-sized paper— 8.3 in. x 11.7 in. (210 mm x 297 mm).

GLUE

Tacky PVA (2)

This type of glue is a great choice for paper flower making, because it's stickier and dries quicker than standard PVA. It still allows for some margin of error and flexibility as it dries clear and doesn't bond instantly, so you can often rearrange flower components as you go. This kind of glue is suitable for all stages of paper flower making and is particularly handy for detail work.

Glue guns (3)

You can get hot-glue guns and cool-melt glue guns. Both work well for this craft. It takes practice not to use too much glue and to avoid leaving strings, so for that reason, along with its instant bond, they are best left to the more confident crafter.

OTHER BASIC MATERIALS

Stems (4)

I use floristry wire for my stems, as it is flexible and easy to cut for arranging. The wire comes in a variety of gauges and finishes.

Floral tape (5)

This is a paper tape that adheres to itself when stretched. It is designed for wrapping floral wire/ stems and attaching multiple stems together. To use the tape, hold the stem(s) to be wrapped at 45 degrees to the end of the tape. Pull the tape to stretch it and activate the wax adhesive. Wrap it around the stem(s), making sure that you overlap as you go, as it will only stick to itself.

BASIC TOOLS

CUTTING

Something to cut your petal shapes is perhaps the most obvious essential tool, but you don't need anything too specialized. All the templates in this book have been designed to consider all equipment availability. You can either hand-cut the flat shapes or use a digital cutting machine (see item 12).

Scissors (6)

Standard paper scissors are perfect for all levels, and it is likely that you already have some at home. The sharper they are, the better.

Scalpel or craft knife (7)

You may already be used to these tools and find them useful for fine, detailed work. Just make sure you cut your paper or card on top of a cutting mat or chopping board, so as not to ruin the table surface underneath.

FOLDING AND FORMING

Pencil and eraser (8)

For tracing the template shapes or drawing your own petal designs onto your chosen paper or card.

Rounded curling tool (9)

I have found that rounded items work as the best tool for curling and forming petals and flower centers. You can use the edge of scissors or flat tools, but rounded tools tend to give a smoother form.

Utilize what you already have at home. My favorites are knitting needles, as they are super smooth, don't bend or snap easily, and come in different gauges, which is useful for all the different flowers. I teach paper flower workshops using wooden skewers: a small piece of wooden dowel or round pencil also works well.

Ruler (10)

A ruler, especially a metal one, is useful to have as a straightedge to score or fold against, particularly for foliage stems.

Pliers (11)

A pair of pliers is really useful for bending the wire used for stems. Pliers are inexpensive, but if you are really stuck without a pair, you can bend most wire thicknesses by hand.

ADDITIONAL TOOLS

CUTTING

Digital cutting machine (12)

I use a digital cutting machine to cut almost all of my flat shapes. They are faster and more accurate than I am at precision cutting! A digital cutting machine takes a file from your computer and plots the shapes on paper. Think of it as a printer that has a small blade, rather than ink.

To use a cutting machine, you place your chosen media onto an adhesive mat that is then fed into a row of rollers that hold it down. The blade moves from left to right, while at the same time the mat is fed back and forth to plot out your shapes.

Fringe scissors

A pair of fringe scissors is a handy tool for use in lots of the flower centers in this book. They are fun, but not essential!

Scallop scissors (13)

If you are hand-cutting your components, some scalloped scissors or pinking shears give a detailed finish to the edges of your pieces. A good example of this design feature is in the Carnation and Daffodil flowers on pages 66 and 59, respectively.

Paper punches (14)

Paper punches punch out small, intricate shapes that would be tricky to hand-cut. The tiny details work well as finishing flourishes in some flower centers.

FOLDING AND FORMING

Ball tools and foam mat (15)

These tools are really useful for making curved/cupped shapes from flat pieces of paper (for example, in the Ranunculus flower on page 70). They can be bought online and aren't overly expensive. If you don't have them, though, try a pencil with a rounded end and dish sponge or mouse mat.

Quilling tool (16)

This little tool is helpful when rolling up vertical flower centers (see page 25). One end of a strip of paper is slotted into the tool, and then you simply twist it in on itself. A good example of where this tool comes into its own is when making the center of the Daisy (see page 57).

Bradawl (17)

This is a sharp point with a handle: piercing holes in paper is made so much easier with a bradawl. You can, of course, use a darning needle or something similar like a metal kebab skewer instead.

Embossing tool (18)

This one is definitely on the "nice to have" list as you can certainly paper craft without one. I use this tool with a ruler for scoring lines in leaves and petals.

Double-sided tape (19)

Sometimes, double-sided tape is easier to work with than glue, particularly when rolling up fringed strips. I also use it on the paper ribbons for the Buttonholes project (see page 120).

Stapler (20)

For speed, a stapler can be another good alternative to glue. Stapling petals is most effective on oversized flowers, as they can take the extra bulk of the staples in a way that smaller flowers can't.

Mini clothespins (21)

Handy for holding components together while the glue dries.

Bone folders (22)

These can be used in so many ways. Some people like to use them for petal forming; this is down to personal preference, and it is worth experimenting to find what works best for you. I also like to use the straight folder to flatten down layers that are glued together: on leaves, for example.

TECHNIQUES TO STUDY

This chapter is intended as a guide to give an overview on how to construct paper flowers. Don't be afraid to deviate and experiment if an idea comes to you while you read.

It is a good idea to read through this chapter and try out each technique, to get an understanding of how each process works. This way you will be setting yourself up for success when you come to try the individual flowers and projects.

FOLDS, BENDS, AND CURLS

There are various ways that paper can be formed in this craft. This photograph shows the four main kinds. Particularly note the white forms below:

1. **Mountain fold**—a fold that goes "up"
2. **Valley fold**—a fold that goes "down"
3. **Bend**—a gentle fold with no crisp line
4. **Curl**—an even looser form than a bend

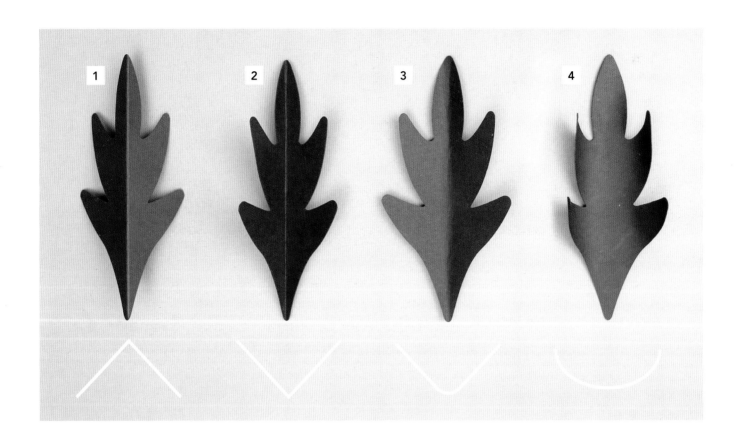

PETALS

Taking flat cut-out shapes and transforming them into 3-D petals is the first step in learning the craft of paper flower making. Once a petal is formed, you can start to build a flower's distinct shape. This is done by varying the number of petals used, by mixing and matching forming methods to add difference, and last, by layering in the center.

To demonstrate petal-forming variations, I have used one petal shape so that you can see how different methods create a range of forms and finished flowers. When you take into account how many different petal shapes you can use, combined with the different forming methods and flower centers, you will see how you could create almost any flower your mind can imagine!

1

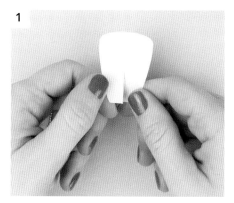

2

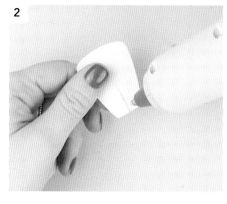

3a

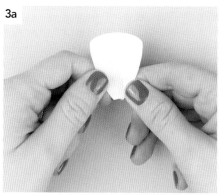

3b

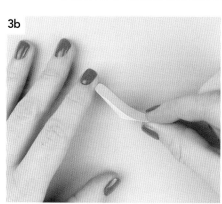

4a

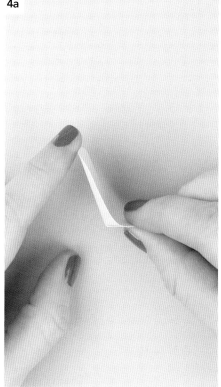

4b

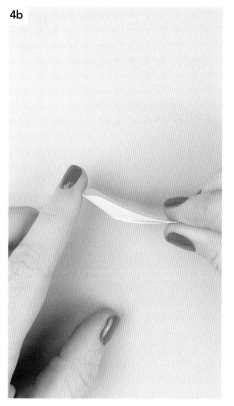

BASIC PETAL CONSTRUCTION

1. Cut a slit at the bottom of the petal to create two tabs.

2. Add glue to one of the tabs.

3a. Lift the other tab over the first; glue together.

3b. Side view
    Altering the length of the cut and subsequent depth of tabs dictates how steep or open the petal will be.

4a. A shorter cut makes a steeper petal and more closed flower.

4b. A longer cut makes a shallower petal and a more open flower.

PETAL FORMING AND SHAPING

There are lots of ways you can shape petals either before or after they have been constructed. Each method gives a different effect and creates a different finished flower. The following are the most useful ways.

1a. Sandwich the petal between your thumb and a curling tool.

1b. Pull the paper along the tool, slightly rotating your working hand as you go. This will curl the full length of the petal.

1c. The petal can curl either outward . . .

1d. or inward (right vs. left).

2. Curl the two corners of the petal outward.

3. Curl the petal vertically, up its length.

4. Pinch the top edge of the petal.

5. With a foam mat and ball tool, crinkle the edge.

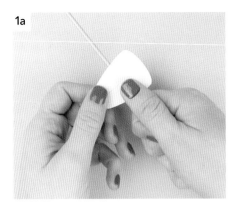

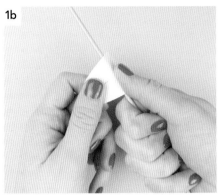

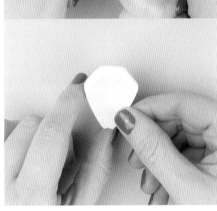

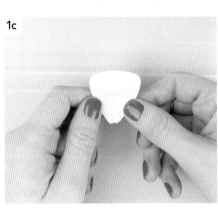

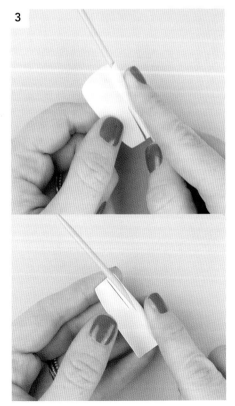

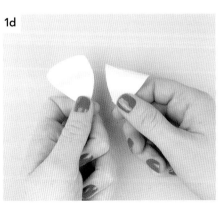

4

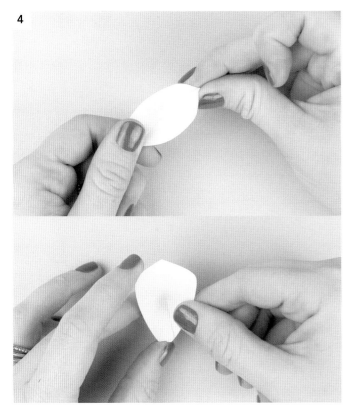

5

BUILDING A FLOWER

Once you have a set of petals, there are four main ways to build a flower, as listed below.

I. Inward

This is when you start with the outer petals on a flat base and work inward, adding the flower center last (e.g., Anemone; see page 50).

II. Outward

When you start with the flower center and build the petals up from the middle, outward (e.g., Ranunculus or Rose; see pages 70 and 86).

III. Layered

2-D layers of connected petals are formed and glued on top of one another to build up the flower head (e.g., Daisy or Dahlia; see pages 56 and 82).

IV. Cone base

These flowers use a cone base (see page 20) rather that starting with a flat base. Petals are added into the cone and built from the outside into the flower center (e.g., Daffodil and Carnation; see pages 59 and 66).

BASES AND COVERS

In this book, I use different bases and base covers. Each has a different function, but the shapes used can overlap these different functions.

Templates are provided at the back of this book for each, in three different sizes, for use in your own flower designs.

DISK / FLAT BASE

This base provides a flat surface on which to attach petals and flower heads to an upright stem. It is the most used base in the "Flowers and Foliage to Master" chapter and is very adaptable. You can build flowers with individual petals or in layers, from the outer petals in, and from the flower center out.

1. Wrap a length of floristry wire in floristry tape.

2. Bend the end of the wire over at 90 degrees.

3. Pierce a hole in the middle of one of the disks.

4. Thread the wire stem through the hole.

5. Add glue over the wire end. A glue gun will give the most secure base.

6. Place the second base shape over the first, securely sandwiching the stem between the two layers. If you aren't using a glue gun, be sure to squeeze the layers together firmly and hold until the glue has dried.

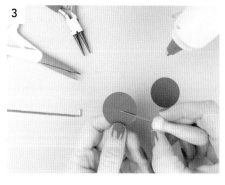

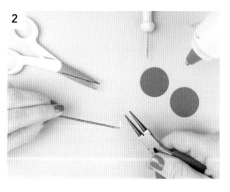

Tip

To make petal spacing easier, use multisided shapes for the stem base: for example, use a pentagon for a five-petal flower. Templates for different shapes can be found at the back of this book.

CONE COVER

This is a simple cone that I use to cover the underside of flowers. Sometimes it goes over an otherwise visible disk / flat base; other times it hides the inner workings of flower construction (see the Rose on page 86).

Cone covers have been provided in the "Templates" section, in two shapes and three sizes.

1. It helps to run a curling tool around the cone to establish the shape.

2. Add glue to the tab and glue into the cone shape.

3. Pierce a hole in the point of the cone.

4. Slide the cone up the stem of the flower and glue in place.

(Full instructions for the flower shown are under Anemone on page 50.)

CONE BASE

The cone base is constructed in exactly the same way as the cone cover, but it has a different function. It provides a shaped base for flowers, with individual petals glued into the inside of the cone. Both the Daffodil and Carnation (see pages 59 and 66) use this construction method, each with different shaped and sized cones.

1. Thread the stem through the cone.

2. Sandwich the end of the stem between the first petal and the cone base, securing in place with glue.

3. Continue around the cone, adding in the remaining petals one at a time.

(Full instructions for assembly of the flower shown are under Carnation, on page 66.)

CUTTING COMPLEX SHAPES

Some of the flowers in this book are built up in layers (see Daisy or Dahlia, pages 56 and 82). For these flowers and some of the centers, I have provided two different template options: you can either cut the full shape out in one layer, or, if you are using thinner paper, you can speed the process up by folding the paper and cutting a quarter of the shape though four layers of paper. This is known as "cutting on the fold."

1

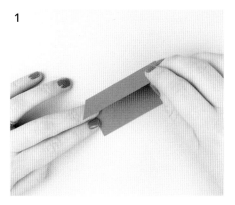

2

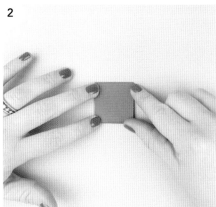

3

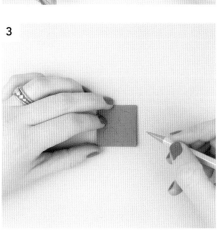

4

5

CUTTING ON THE FOLD

1. Cut a square of paper slightly larger than the desired finished shape, and fold it in half.

2. Fold it in half again.

3. Line up the point of the template with the corner that is all folds—i.e., the side that has no paper edges.

4. Cut around the shape (indicated by the dashed line on the relevant templates, making sure not to cut the right-angled point (indicated by the solid line).

5. Unfold.

CENTERS

The flower centers I use fall into two categories: vertical or horizontal. There are lots of suitable shapes you can use for each, and many combinations that can be built together.

Horizontal center—a flat shape that is formed and then glued into a flower, using the base of the shape for structure

Vertical center—a rolled center that is glued in an upright position

You will find that different centers work best in different flowers. This section covers the basic forming methods: you'll see how they can be adapted for alternative effects when you move on to the individual flower tutorials.

The templates for this section can be found at the back of this book.

HORIZONTAL CENTER I

There are several ways to form this shape, as shown below.

1. **Curled**—Run a curling tool down each stamen, starting from the middle. It may take a few strokes to form the curve. You can gently manipulate the paper with your hands to even out the shape.

2. **Folded**—Fold each stamen into the middle of the shape, then fold the round ends back in the opposite direction.

3. **Rolled**—Place the piece on a foam mat and run a ball tool around the base of the shape. Continue until a slight bend is formed and the stamens gently stand up.

4. Curled, folded, and rolled centers next to each other for comparison

1

2

3

4

HORIZONTAL CENTER II

This shape lends itself to different forming methods.

1. **Folded and curled**—Fold the stamen into the middle of the shape, then tightly curl the tips outward.

2. **Curled**—Curl (rather than fold) the stamens inward. Notice that this is the same method as Horizontal Center I, curled variation, but gives a very different effect due to the different flat shape used.

3. **Tight curl**—Roll each stamen around a curling tool, starting from the ends and working inward; this gives a much tighter curl.

4. The three different results from the horizontal curling: folded and curled, curled, and tight curl at the bottom

1

2

3

4

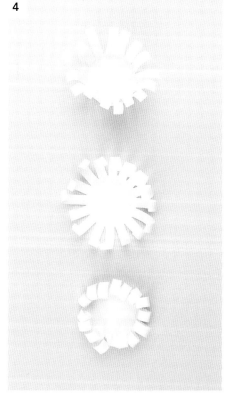

1

2

3

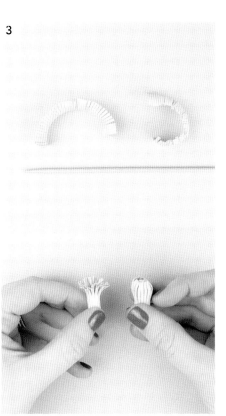

4

VERTICAL CENTERS

Vertical centers are formed and rolled to create a component piece that can be glued on its end into the middle of a flower (i.e., vertically).

1. **Outward curl**—Curl the full length of the fringing with a round tool and then roll it so that the curl is directed outward. Fix the end with glue.

2. **Inward curl**—Curl the tips of the fringing and roll it in the opposite direction to the previous example, so that each curl is directed inward. Fix the end with glue.

3. **Short**—Try both of these methods with different sizes and lengths of fringed strip.

4. The four different results for comparison: long outward, long inward, short outward, and short inward.

BLOOMS TO PRACTICE

This section features some basic step-by-step instructions that apply the techniques outlined in the previous chapter to create full flowers. Each demonstrates the attributes you can vary to create different flowers:

- number of petals
- number of petal layers
- size of petals
- open and closed flowers
- petal-forming varieties
- flower-center combinations

These blooms are a good way to experiment and practice flower making and find your preferred methods, tools, and papers.

These flowers have been given names to identify them, but they are all more stylized than they are realistic. This makes them a great starting point for a beginner.

The templates for these flowers detail how many of each component you will need to trace and cut out. The templates can be found at the back of this book, starting on page 146. There are also some alternative petals and centers to test out.

CAMELLIA

This flower uses six petals over two layers. They have a mid-sized cut. The center is built up of three different, inward-curled, horizontal components, and the flower is constructed from the outer petal, inward.

A variation of this flower features in the Chandelier guided project, later in this book (see page 113).

1. Curl the petals outward.

2. Overlap the petal tabs.

3. Glue three of the petals into a rough triangle on the base. (You could use a shaped base to get a more even spread.)

4. Add the remaining three petals in the gaps between the first layer.

5. Curl the largest central piece inward.

6. Glue the curled center into the middle of the flower, then repeat with the smaller piece.

7. Roll the fringed disk from the outer edge in toward the middle. This gives a tighter curl than on the previous two layers.

8. Manipulate the center with your hands to even out the shape, then glue it into the middle of the flower.

9. Add the flower head to a disk base and finish with a cone cover.

1

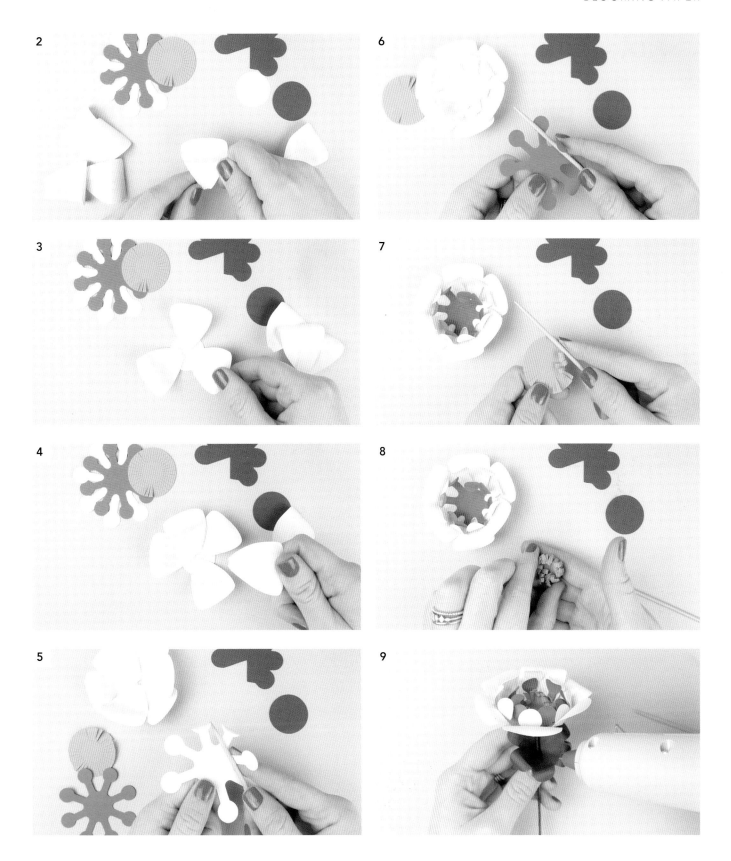

FRITILLARIA

This flower features four petals with a short cut, making the final bloom tighter and more closed than the Camellia. There is one folded, horizontal center, and one outward-curled, vertical center.

I used this flower in the Table Arrangement guided project on page 131.

1. Fold the petals in half, lengthways.

2. Glue the petal tabs.

3. Curl the corners outward.

4. Glue the petals to the base.

5

8

6

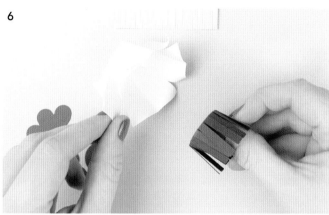

9

7

10

5. Fold the flower center inward at the base of each stamen.

6. Glue the center into the middle of the petals.

7. Curl the vertical center / fringed strip.

8. Roll the strip so that the fringing curls outward.

9. Add glue to the rolled end and add to the middle of the flower.

10. Add a disk base and cone cover.

LILY

This example uses an odd number of petals. I have used a pentagon-shaped base as a guide to ensure the petal spacing is even. The five petals have a long cut to give an open flower, and they have no other forming methods. The center is made up of the same components as the Fritillaria but is formed differently, demonstrating how you can get different effects with the same shapes.

1. Glue the formed petals onto the base, centering each on a side of the pentagon.

2. Curl the two horizontal centers and glue into the flower middle, offsetting them from each other.

3. Curl the vertical fringed center.

4. Roll the fringing, with the curl directed outward.

5. Glue into the center of the flower and add a disk base / cone cover.

2

4

3

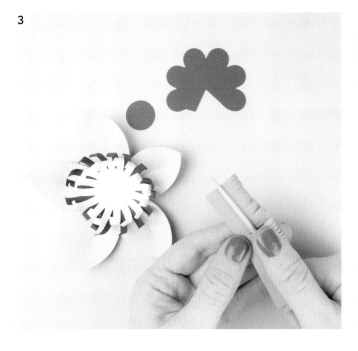

5

BUTTERCUP

This flower doesn't feature individual petals like the others in this section; instead, there are horizontal petal layers that are formed and added to each other. For this flower, a base isn't needed, as the wire stem can be sandwiched between the petal layers. The middle of the flower features another horizontal layer and a vertical, inwardly curled center.

This flower features in the Table Arrangement (on page 131), Chandelier (page 113), and Cake Topper (page 110) projects.

1. Curl the petal layers inward.

2. Pierce a hole in one of the petal layers and thread through a wire stem with a 90-degree bend (as would be done on a standard disk / flat base).

3. Glue the next petal layer on top, sandwiching the bent end of the wire. The petals on the second layer should sit offset between those on the first.

4. Slide the cone cover up the stem.

5. Curl the horizontal centers inward.

6. Glue the two layers together, offsetting them from each other.

7. Curl center 2 and roll so that the petals are directed inward.

8. Glue the centers into the middle of the flower.

3

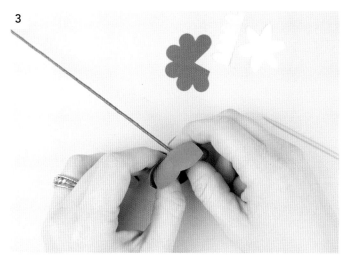

6

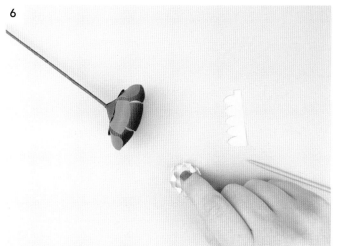

4

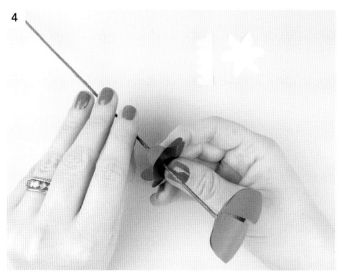

7

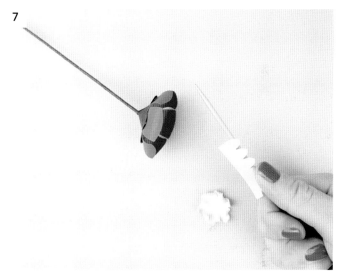

5

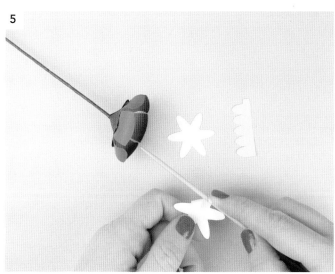

8

DESIGNS TO INSPIRE

Designing new blooms is one of the most satisfying processes for me. I don't aim to replicate nature but rather use it as inspiration. My flowers are intentionally stylized and graphic rather than hyperrealistic.

My collection has been informed by fresh flowers but also botanical illustrations, fabric design, graphic design, and product packaging. I experiment with shapes and layering (as in the previous chapters) to bring my ideas into reality.

Now that we have gone through the basic techniques, this chapter will illustrate how you can apply them to your own flower designs, inspired by what you see around you. Perhaps you have a favorite art print or floral fabric with sentimental value that might spark an idea?

GRAPHIC DESIGN AND ILLUSTRATION: A MEADOW FLOWER

I have extracted shapes from this vintage botanical illustration and designed a stylized version of the flower and a foliage stem. The instructions for the foliage are shown under Meadow Flower Foliage on page 100.

This Meadow Flower also features in the Chandelier and Table Arrangement guided projects (see pages 113 and 131).

EXTRACTING THE SHAPES

Trace the petal and leaf shapes, mirroring them to ensure the final petal is symmetrical and elongating the traced shape to allow for the angles of the drawing. The process is shown in the illustration above.

You don't need to do this because templates have been provided (see page 146). But keep this page open while you make the flower, so that you can see where the design came from.

1. Overlap the petal tabs to create the basic petal form.

2. Curl back the petal corners.

3

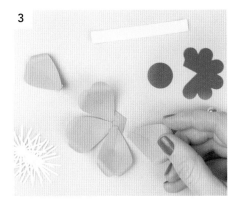

7

4

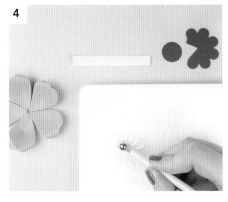

8

5

9

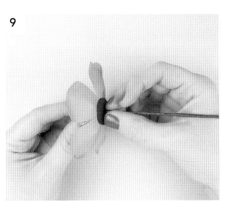

6

10

3. Glue the petals to the base, centering each to a side of the pentagon.

4. Run a ball tool around the middle of the horizontal flower centers (or gently fold/bend them up).

5. Layer up the flower center, offsetting the layers from each other.

6. Curl the fringed strip.

7. Roll the fringed strip so that the curl is directed inward.

8. Add this to the middle of the flower.

9. Glue the flower to the disk base.

10. Add a cone cover to hide the base.

FRESH FLOWERS: A GARDEN ROSE

Using fresh garden roses as inspiration demanded a slightly different approach to the previous botanical illustration. I started by studying the flower head, drawing it, taking photographs, deconstructing it, and hand-cutting paper versions of the petals.

The petal shapes were scanned into the computer, traced, and sent to my digital cutting machine to make a first mock-up of the rose. It took four further mock-ups before I reached the final version of my Garden Rose.

Full instructions for making this flower can be found in "Flowers and Foliage to Master" on page 91.

1.   pencil study of the fresh flowers
2a–b. hand-cut experimentation
3.   deconstructing the petal layers
4.   scanned and traced petals
5a–b. petals on digital cutting machine
6.   final flower templates
7.   Garden Rose mock-ups

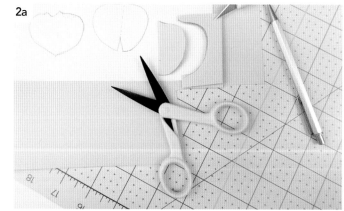

2a

1

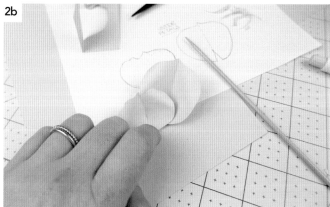

2b

3

5b

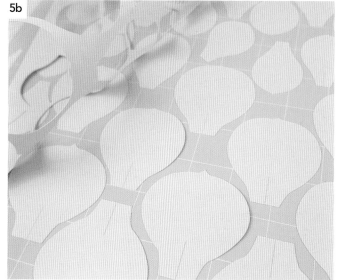

4

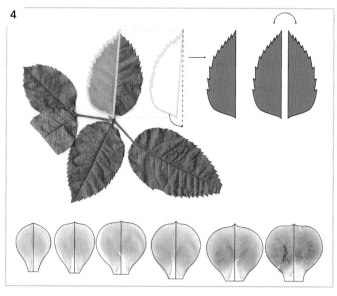

6

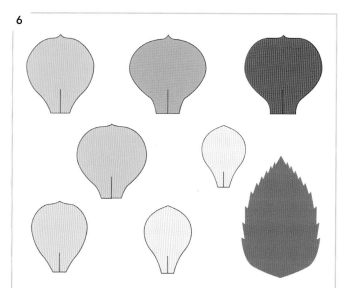

5a

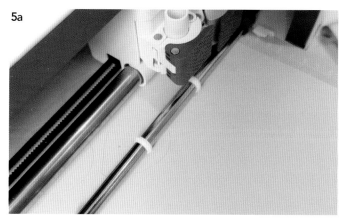

7

FLOWERS AND FOLIAGE TO MASTER

This is where the fun starts! If you have skipped straight to this section, it's a good idea to cast a quick eye over the techniques chapter to familiarize yourself with the basics.

Practice these flowers to get a clear understanding of how to build them. It's a good idea to save any special papers until you have done at least one practice run. If you do have a particular sheet in mind, try to use a similar-weight paper for your practice flowers so that you can see how it might behave.

This section also features four examples of foliage that you can adapt to complement your floral displays. Experiment by mixing and matching the shapes with the different construction methods.

And remember, "It's not wrong, it's different."

You will find the full templates for these flowers and foliage stems at the back of this book (see page 146). Trace the templates (by hand or digitally) and cut out all components, as detailed on the templates. I will run through each step by step and give a difficulty rating along with hints and tips at the start of each tutorial.

As a quick reiteration of the different ways paper flowers can be built, this book explores four variations:

I. Inward
This is when you start with the outer petals on a flat base and work inward, adding the flower center last (see Anemone on page 50).

II. Outward
When you start with the flower center and build the petals up from the middle, outward (see Ranunculus or Rose on pages 70 and 86).

III. Layered
2-D layers of connected petals are formed and glued on top of one another to build the flower head (see Daisy or Dahlia on pages 56 and 82).

IV. Cone base
These flowers use a cone base (see "Techniques to Study" on page 20) rather that starting with a flat base. Petals are added into the cone and built from the outside into the flower center (see Daffodil or Carnation on pages 59 and 66).

PEONY BUD

Difficulty: Very simple
Base type: Formed flat base
Build type: Layered

These little filler buds are great for a multitude of reasons: they are easy to make and a great way to add pops of color to floral designs, and the pieces are small enough to be cut from the offcuts or scraps left over from making a larger bloom. They work well in clusters (see the Table Arrangement on page 131) or on their own in delicate items such as Buttonholes (see page 120).

Peony buds are constructed in a similar way to the Peony flower (see page 53)—in curled layers. They work well in stylized or realistic displays, and you can use any paper or card that you fancy for them.

TOOLS AND MATERIALS

- ball tools—optional
- bradawl or darning needle
- curling tool
- floristry wire for the stems
- foam mat—optional
- glue—any type
- paper—scraps or offcuts
- pliers—needlenose are best
- scissors, knife, or digital cutting machine

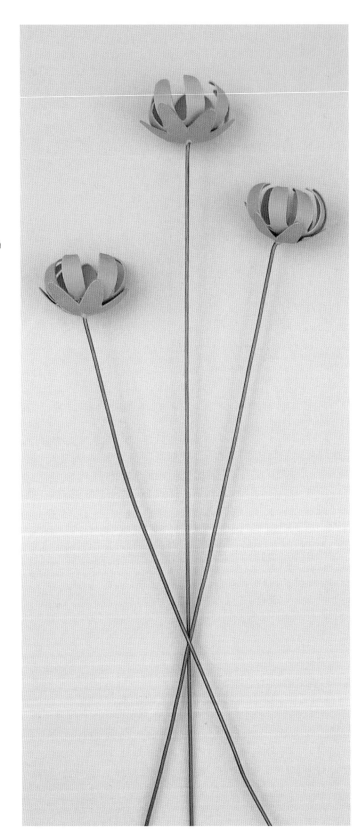

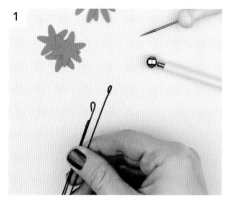

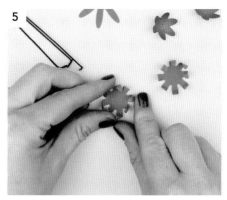

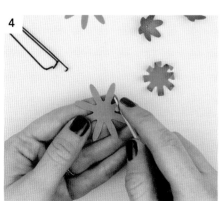

1. At the ends of the floristry wire, bend small loops at 90 degrees to the main stem.

2. Run a ball tool around the base layers in a circular motion—I'm making three bases simultaneously here.

3. Pierce holes in the centers of the base layers.

4. Curl the petals of the top layers inward toward the middle of the flowers.

5. Gently manipulate the curls with your fingers to even out the shape.

6. Run a ball tool around the middle of the petal layers. The shape matches the cup shape of the base layer.

7. Thread the wire stem through the pierced hole and add glue.

8. Sandwich the looped wire end between the base layer and petal layer. If you want, you can add a second petal layer.

BILLY BUTTONS

Difficulty: Simple
Base type: No base
Build type: Layered

This little flower was designed especially for this book. It's a simple layered construction that works well as filler in floral arrangements. It is easy to hand-cut, as the base shapes are simple and have no curves! Billy Buttons bring texture and pops of color to any arrangement.

Billy Buttons are built up in flat, formed layers, in the same way as the Dahlia, Daisy, and Peony. Just like the former, there are quite a few petals to form, but the final result is worth the time involved.

You can use any paper or card for this little pom-pom, although I would steer clear of anything really thick for your first attempt, as it can be a bit fiddly.

I've used the basic pom-pom shape of this flower in several of the guided projects, including the Table Arrangement (see page 131) and Chandelier (see page 113).

TOOLS AND MATERIALS

- bradawl or darning needle
- curling tool
- floristry wire—1 long piece for the stem
- glue (any kind)
- paper—under a quarter of an A4 sheet
- scissors, knife, or digital cutting machine

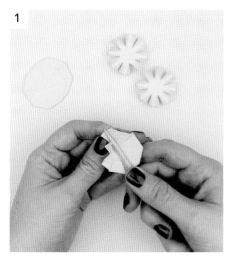

1. Hold a straight curling tool directly through the middle of each of the sides of the octagonal petal layer, and bend the section up around it. This makes the next step much easier.

2. Pinch and fold the bend from the outside edge.

3. Snip the corners off each petal.

4. Curl two of the three fringed centers.

5. Roll the first with the curl directed inward, and secure the end with glue.

6. Wrap the second around the first, but with the curl directed outward. Secure with glue.

7. Wrap the third fringed strip around a straight curling tool to give a tighter curl than the previous strips.

8. Add the final layer to the center so that the fringe is directed outward.

9. Gently fold the petals of the first layer upward.

10. Glue the fringed center into the middle of the first petal layer.

11. Repeat step 9 on the next petal layer. Then add it underneath the first layer. Offset so that the petals fill the gaps between those in the first layer.

12. Repeat on two more petal layers. From the side, you will now have a flat bottom and curved top.

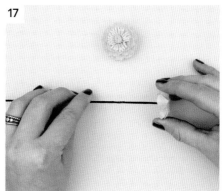

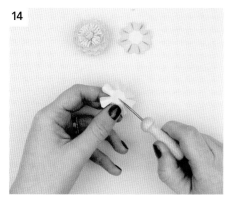

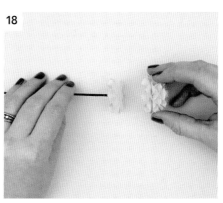

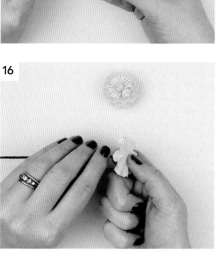

13. As you add the next two layers, gently fold back the petals in the opposite direction to step 9.

14. Pierce a hole in the middle of one of the remaining two layers.

15. Thread a stem, with a bent end, through the hole.

16. Glue the remaining layer over the wire end, firmly sandwiching it to create the flower's base. Be sure that the petals are offset from each other between the layers.

17. Gently push the petals down toward the stem. Be careful not to push too hard and flatten the folding.

18. Line the two sections up so that the layers that are about to meet are offset from each other.

19. Glue the two sections together.

ANEMONE

Difficulty: Simple
Base type: Disk base—flat
Build type: Inward

This is a variation on the very first paper flower I designed, and it is a really good one to start with, as the construction is straightforward, it's not too intricate, and there aren't lots of components to cut out. You can use most paper weights for this flower. I suggest beginning with a medium weight and experimenting to find your preferred media.

This flower looks impressive when finished. Its open, flat design works in effective contrast with more closed flowers like the Tulip, or more textured ones like Rose and Carnation. This makes the Anemone a good choice for a range of floral projects.

I used the Anemone in a very pale lilac in the Bouquet project (page 124) and supersized it for the Garland project (page 128). Due to its simple construction, this flower works particularly well at larger scales.

TOOLS AND MATERIALS

- bradawl or darning needle
- curling tool
- disk base
- floristry tape
- floristry wire—1 long piece for the stem, 1 shorter piece for the leaf
- glue gun—optional
- paper—as required for bases, leaves, and centers. Under half an A4 sheet for the petals
- PVA glue
- scissors, knife, or digital cutting machine

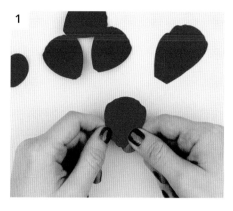

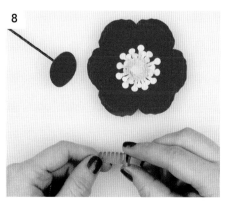

1. Overlap and glue the petal tabs to form the basic petal shape.

2. Holding the bottom tip, curl the very top edge of each petal outward.

3. Glue three of the petals onto the base, aiming for a rough triangle. Then glue the next three on top, filling in the gaps between the first three.

4. Run a small ball tool around each of the three centers. Alternatively, bend them in by hand.

5. Glue center 1 into the middle of the flower, followed by center 2—offset these layers from each other, as shown. You can gently rearrange the stamens at this stage.

6. Layer in the two fringed disks (center 3).

7. Curl the tips of center 4.

8. Roll, with the curls directed inward, and secure with glue.

9. Add it to the middle of the flower.

10. Add the disk base.

11. Fold back the petals of the cone cover.

12. It is most effective to place the cone cover so that each of the flower petals in the first layer sits centrally over a pair of the base cone's leaves. Then glue each petal of the cone cover to the underside of the flower head.

13. Sandwich the short piece of floristry wire between the two leaf layers. Tacky/quick-drying PVA is best here, as it is more forgiving and less bulky than a glue gun.

14. Before the glue has dried, gently curl the leaf.

15. Using floristry tape, attach the leaf to the stem.

PEONY

Difficulty: Simple
Base type: Disk base—flat
Build type: Layered

This flower has remained pretty much unchanged over the many years that I have been making it. It's a great one to add to displays as it has a distinct rounded shape and brings a loose softness.

The Peony is a layered flower in the same way as the Daisy, Dahlia, and Billy Buttons, but there are fewer layers and the petals are shaped in a totally different way from these other flowers.

This is one of the quickest flowers to make in the book, and when it comes to choice of materials, you can be led by what you like the look of; any weight will work! If you are hand-cutting and want to use the "cut on the fold" method for cutting the main shape, a lighter-weight paper will be easier—but you can always cut each petal individually to be able to use a dream color in a heavier weight.

I use this flower in the Table Arrangement project (page 131), for the Wreath (page 106) and the Chandelier (page 113). You'll see it in different colorways in each project. If you are designing your own arrangement, a nice effect is matching the center details to another flower's petals.

TOOLS AND MATERIALS

- bradawl or darning needle
- curling tool
- disk base
- floristry tape
- floristry wire—1 long piece for the stem
- paper—as required for bases, leaves, and centers; 1 A4 sheet for the petals
- PVA glue and optional glue gun
- scissors, knife, or digital cutting machine

1. Run a curling tool down each petal, from the flower middle to the petal tip.

2. The petals curl into the middle of each layer.

3. Gently manipulate the petals to even out the shape.

4. Glue two layers together, slightly offsetting them as shown.

5. Add the third layer, filling the remaining gaps between petals.

6. A gentle squeeze to the petals will ensure the shape is kept even.

7. Fold up the stamen of each center piece.

8. Then fold the rounded end out in the opposite direction.

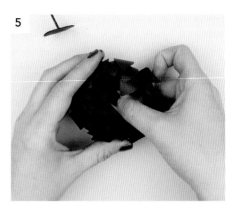

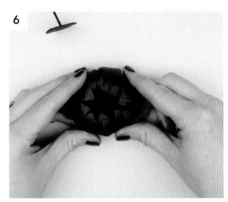

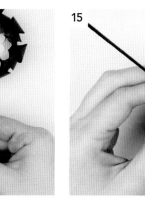

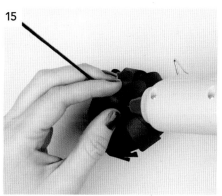

9. Glue center 2 into the middle of center 1 (the smaller into the larger one). Offset them so that the smaller stamens fill the spaces between the larger. Glue them into the middle of the flower.

10. Curl the fringed centers.

11. Roll the first center so that the curl is directed inward. Secure the end with glue.

12. Roll the second center around the first, so that the fringe curls outward. Secure the end with glue.

13. Add the fringed centers into the middle of the flower.

14. Glue a disk base onto the bottom of the flower.

15. Add a cone cover to finish the flower.

DAISY

Difficulty: Simple
Base type: Disk base—flat
Build type: Layered

A playful, springtime flower that is deceptively easy to make, the Daisy is a flat, layered bloom, constructed in the same way as the Peony. In fact, they use very similar petal shapes, but completely different forming methods.

While the technique is straightforward, a little patience is needed for this one, as it can be a bit time consuming. The payoff is worth it though!

I am often asked how I manage to make the daisy centers: read on to see the simplicity of it.

As with the previous two flowers, any paper will work with the Daisy: it is a good one to experiment with, to find what material you like working with.

I used daisies in the Bouquet (page 124), Buttonholes (page 120), and Table Arrangement (page 131), as well as without stems for the Chandelier (page 113), and Cake Topper (page 110).

TOOLS AND MATERIALS

- bradawl or darning needle
- curling tool
- disk base
- floristry wire—1 long piece for the stem
- glue—any kind
- paper—as required for bases, leaves, and centers under half an A4 sheet for the petals
- quilling tool—optional
- scissors, knife, or digital cutting machine

1

4

2

5

3

6

1. Place a thin curling tool down the length of each petal, and bend the petal around the tool.

2. Glue two layers together, centrally offsetting them so that the petals of one sit between the petals of the other.

3. Add the next two layers. Again, distribute the petals evenly.

4. Curl the fringe strip around the tool.

5. Roll the fringed strip with the curl directed outward. A quilling tool is handy for this step, but not essential.

6. Secure the end with glue.

7

10

8

11

9

7. Mold the center with your fingers, curling the edges down and round.

8. Glue the center into the middle of the flower.

9. Add the disk base.

10. Slide the cone cover up the stem.

11. Push the cone cover up so that the flower closes slightly, then glue it in place.

DAFFODIL

Difficulty: Average
Base type: Cone base
Build type: Inward

This is a happy little flower—its arrival is one of the first signs of spring in the UK. The Daffodil is constructed by inserting individual petals into a cone base, which is finished with its unique trumpeted center. Like the Carnation (see page 66), if you are hand-cutting your flowers, a pair of scalloped scissors or pinking shears will work well on the top edge of the central trumpeted section.

It is a good idea to make sure the base cone is the same thickness (or thicker) as the paper you plan to use for the petals, as the cone is quite small, in comparison, to the final flower.

I like to use this bloom in more stylized displays: I used white-on-white versions in my Table Arrangement project (page 131).

TOOLS AND MATERIALS

- bradawl or darning needle
- curling tool
- floristry wire—1 long piece for the stem
- glue—any type
- paper—as required for bases, leaves, and center under half an A4 sheet for the petals
- quilling tool—optional
- scalloped scissors or pinking sheers—optional
- scissors, knife, or digital cutting machine

1. Curl the petals inward, vertically.

2. Pinch the narrow point of each petal.

3. Thread a straight piece of floristry wire through the base cone. Center it within one of the leaf sections, as shown.

4. Glue the first petal over the wire, firmly sandwiching the wire between it and the base cone. A glue gun will give the strongest bond for this, so if you are using a glue that dries less quickly, be sure to hold the pieces for a minute or two.

5. Continue around the base, gluing in the other five petals. Each petal should be centered over a leaf on the base cone. The petals will overlap each other.

6. Ensure the petals overlap in the correct order—the right-hand edge of each should overlap the left-hand edge of the one it sits beside.

7. Curl the central trumpet section of the Daffodil.

8. Bring the edges together.

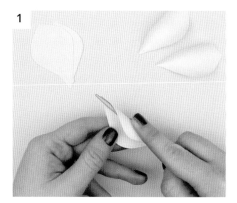

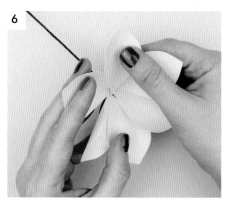

9. Apply glue to the inner side of the tab (the join will be less visible this way), and glue into its trumpet shape.

10. Turn the trumpet cone section over and gently push the tips of the cone inward.

11. Apply glue to the tips.

12. Glue the trumpet section into the middle of the flower.

13. Curl the fringed center.

14. Roll the fringing so that the curl is directed outward. A quilling tool can help here, as it's quite small and this rolling can be fiddly.

15. Glue it into the center of the Daffodil.

16. Add a line of glue down the middle of the leaves at one end. Quick-dry PVA works best for this step as it's less bulky than a glue gun and will dry clear.

17. Glue the leaves to the stem, sandwiching a small section of the stem between the two leaves.

TULIP

Difficulty: Average
Base type: Formed flat base
Build type: Inward

Natural tulips come in so many different colors, which makes them a great design inspiration. Of course, if you are making your own paper blooms, the colors available in nature do not restrict you!

The Tulip's shape is unlike any other flower in this book, which means that it makes an important addition to displays as it brings its own texture with the upward direction of its petals.

The construction of a Tulip is most similar to the Anemone in that each of the six petals is individually formed and attached to a central base. Comparing the two is a good example of how changing the petal forming, by altering the cut depth and curl direction, can give you a completely different flower, despite the construction or component parts being very similar.

This is another flower that works well in a variety of paper thicknesses. It is one to experiment with and find your preferred material.

I used tulips in the display for the cover and also for the Bouquet (page 124) and in the Window Display project at the end of the book (page 138).

TOOLS AND MATERIALS

- ball tools—or substitutes; see "Materials" and "Tools"
- bradawl or darning needle
- curling tool
- floristry tape
- floristry wire—one long piece for the stem
- foam mat or similar

- glue gun—optional
- paper—as required for bases, leaves, and centers under half an A4 sheet for the petals
- PVA glue
- scissors, knife, or digital cutting machine

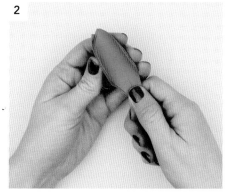

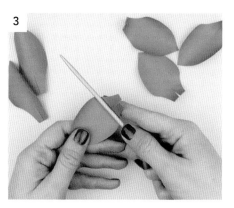

1. Curl all petals inward, vertically up the petal.

2. Stack the petals together and gently squeeze them to make sure the curve is even across all of them.

3. Gently holding the tip of each petal, place the curling tool parallel with the flat end of the petal.

4. Curl the flat end inward.

5. Overlap the two tabs and glue the petal form. Add just a small dot of glue near the tip of the tabs in order to maintain the curls you made in steps 3 and 4.

6. Run a ball tool up each leaf on the base pieces. This creates a cupped shape.

7. Pierce a hole in one of the two base pieces.

8

10

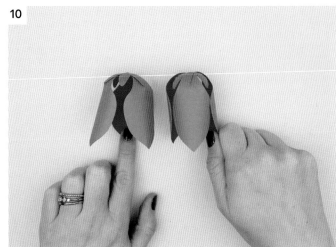

9

11

8. On the cupped-base piece with the hole, glue three petals on the inside. Place a petal on one of the leaves of the cupped base, then leave the next blank. Add another petal on the one after that, leave the next blank, and add the third on the next. Every other leaf should have a petal centered on it (study the photo for detail).

9. Glue the remaining three petals to the underside of the cupped-base piece that does not have a pierced hole. Again, center them on every other base leaf.

10. The layer without the pierced hole goes inside the layer with the pierced hole. The layers are offset from each other, so that the petals on the inner layer fill the spaces between the petals on the outer layer, as shown.

11. Thread the stem wire (with a bent-over end, like the standard disk bases) through the pierced hole, and sandwich it between the two flower layers.

12

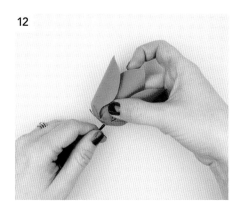

16

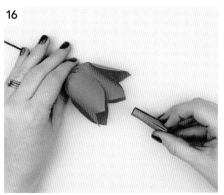

12. Glue down the free cupped-base leaves on the outside of the tulip.

13. The inner petals should sit in the gaps between the outer layer's petals.

13

17

14. Curl the tips of the fringed center.

15. Roll the fringed center with the curled top directed inward. Secure with glue.

16. Glue the stamen into the middle of the flower.

14

18

17. From the tip, add a line of glue, an inch or so long, down the middle of the leaf.

18. Stick the leaf to the flower stem. Quick-dry PVA works best for this step as it's less bulky than a glue gun and will dry clear.

15

19

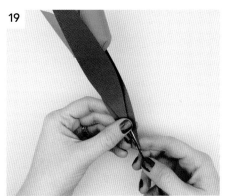

19. Repeat with the second leaf on the other side of the stem.

CARNATION

Difficulty: Average
Base type: Cone base
Build type: Inward, cone

This flower brings a frilly softness to any arrangement or project, and it sits really well in both stylized and realistic designs. If you're hand-cutting your flowers, a pair of scalloped scissors or pinking shears would work well on the top edges of the petals. You could also cut a smooth curve or try tearing the edges. This is a perfect example of "It's not wrong, it's different."

I used these flowers in the Table Arrangement project (page 131). For that display, I used a velum (tracing paper) for the petals. I would recommend starting with thinner paper, rather than heavier paper or card, as fitting the petals into the base can be a bit of a squeeze with thicker materials.

TOOLS AND MATERIALS

- bradawl or darning needle
- curling tool
- floristry wire—1 long piece for the stem
- glue—any kind
- paper—as required for cone base; 1 A4 sheet of paper for the petals
- scalloped scissors or pinking shears—optional
- scissors, knife, or digital cutting machine

1. Put a vertical bend down the center of each petal 1.

2. Curl the two edges of the petals outward from the vertical bend.

3. Pinch the point of each petal.

4. Thread a straight piece of floristry wire through the cone base, and center it within one of the cone's leaves, as shown.

5. Glue the first petal over the wire, firmly sandwiching the wire between it and the base cone. A glue gun will give the strongest bond for this, so if you're using something that dries less quickly, be sure to hold the pieces together for a minute or two until they are fully dry.

6. Continue around the base, centering the remaining five petal 1 pieces in the base cone leaves. Depending on how tight you have bent and curled the petals, there may be some overlap.

7. Repeat the same petal forming and shaping with all the petal 2 pieces.

8. Curl the point of petal 2 inward; the curled tip is where you add the glue for the second layer of petals.

9. Glue these petals centrally over the joins between each of the petals in the previous layer underneath.

10. The petals in this layer will overlap each other.

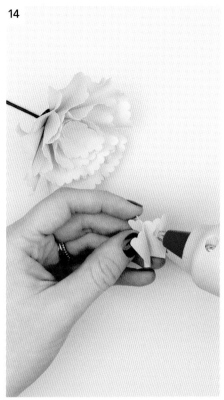

11. Curl the three petals that make up the next layer, inward and vertically.

12. Glue them into the center of the flower, overlapping every other join between petals in the previous layer. As there is less room in the middle for your fingers by this stage, you may find it useful to use a tool to push the petal into the flower.

13. The last layer of petals are also curled vertically. Fold the tip of the petal inward to provide more of a surface for gluing.

14. Glue these final three petals back to back in a triangle.

15. And finally, glue them into the center of the flower.

RANUNCULUS

Difficulty: Advanced
Base type: Disk base—flat
Build type: Outward

Ranunculus flowers are known for their delicate layered heads and are popular with florists and clients alike. I first made this flower for my sister's wedding bouquet. It is built up of the simplest and most basic of all shapes: a series of circles.

There is a lot of crinkling to do, so a set of ball-forming tools and a foam mat will make this task a breeze. If you don't have these, try a pencil with a rounded end, and a mouse pad, or dish sponge, or simply leave the edges uncrinkled.

This flower is built from the center, outward. I tend to favor mid-weight papers for this bloom. The thickness of the paper will affect the amount of pressure you have to apply to crinkle the edges, so a little experimentation before you start is a good idea.

I used this flower in both the Bouquet (see page 124) and the Buttonholes (see page 120) projects, and it features on the cover. Ranunculus work particularly well in designs that have a realistic aesthetic, as they add texture to displays and they suit accent or bright colors due to their relatively small, closed head.

TOOLS AND MATERIALS

- ball tools—or substitutes; see "Materials" and "Tools"
- bradawl or darning needle
- curling tool
- disk base
- floristry tape
- floristry wire—1 long piece for the stem, 3 shorter pieces for leaves
- foam mat or similar
- glue—any type
- paper—as required for bases, leaves, and centers under an A4 sheet for the petals
- scissors, knife, or digital cutting machine

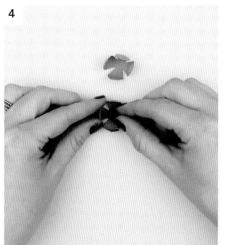

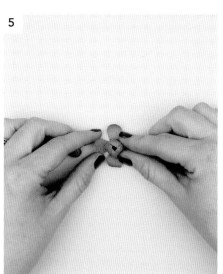

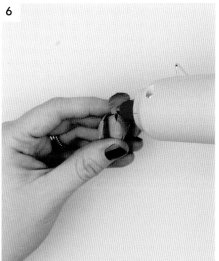

1. Curl the tips of the center.

2. Roll the center so that the curls are directed inward, and secure the end with glue.

3. Run a ball tool around the edges of each of the inner petals. I like to use a tool that is slightly smaller in diameter than the width of the petal.

4. Glue the center into the middle of the first inner petal layer.

5. Fold the petals around the center and glue them to each other. Glue this piece onto the next inner petal layer.

6. Add glue at the base of each petal on the second layer, then fold the petals up, around the inner section.

7

9

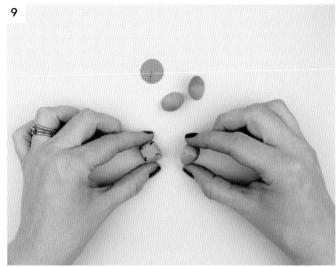

8

10

7. Crinkle the edges of the flat shapes by running a ball tool around the edge of the petals—working your way inward in a spiral motion.

8. All the petals from this layer onward are made in the same way—by overlapping the edges on either side of the cut-out segment. The petal shapes vary slightly—each segment is proportionally different—and that is what dictates how open or closed the layer will be.

9. Turn the middle of the flower over and glue the four petal 4 pieces onto each corner: the petals will overlap each previous petal as you go around the flower.

10. Add petal 3 pieces to the flower. Center them over the overlap between two petals on the previous layer.

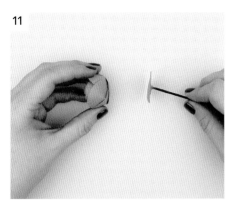

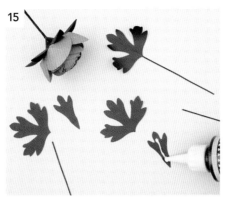

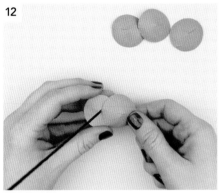

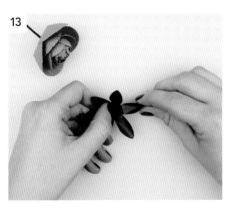

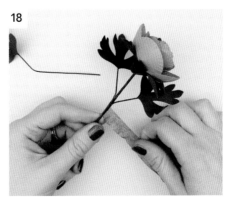

11. Glue the flower to the disk base.

12. Add the final layer of petals over the base. Again, center these petals between the petal overlaps on the previous layer. You can also add in another layer at this stage (see the templates).

13. Bend the leaves of the cone base along their length, and pinch the points.

14. Add the cone cover to the flower.

15. Add glue to the leaf back.

16. Sandwich one of the short pieces of wire between the leaf back and leaf.

17. Curl the leaf before the glue has completely dried.

18. Use floristry tape to fix the leaves to the main stem.

FREESIA

Difficulty: Advanced
Base type: No base!
Build type: Series of cones

These stems are quite fiddly to make, but they make such a difference to a floral arrangement. Each flower head is made up of two nesting mini cones (holding the petals) and a center that mimics the natural flower while also concealing the construction. On that note, be sure to pay attention to where the tabs need to be glued!

As each flower head is quite small, it's a good idea to use lighter-weight paper rather than card. Avoid thicker stem wire—go for a 22 gauge, approximately. Try enlarging the templates to practice this bloom.

I have used this stem in the Bouquet (see page 124) as it gives a lovely, loose shape to the finished arrangement. It also features on the cover photograph.

TOOLS AND MATERIALS

- bradawl or darning needle
- curling tool
- floristry tape
- floristry wire—1 long piece, 5 shorter pieces
- glue—any type
- paper—as required for bases, leaves, and centers under half an A4 sheet for the petals
- scissors, knife, or digital cutting machine

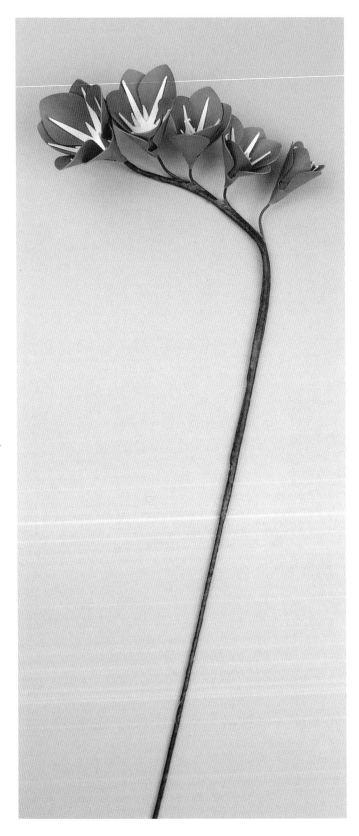

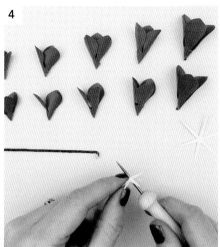

1. Lay your curling tool down each petal and bend the petals around the tool.

2. For each size, glue the tab of one of the petal cones on the outside.

3. And glue one tab on the inside —repeat for each sized pair.

4. Pierce a hole through the middle of the smaller center piece in each pair. Bend over the end of the wire, and thread the other end through the hole.

5. Glue the larger center piece over the top of the smaller, firmly sandwiching the bent wire end between the two layers. A glue gun will give the strongest base, but requires some practice to use the small amount needed. If you're using another glue, be sure to hold these pieces for a minute or two, until they are fully dry.

6. Fold up the center pieces away from the stem.

7

8

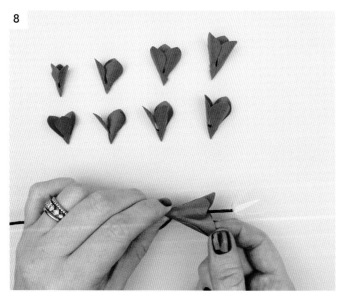

9

10

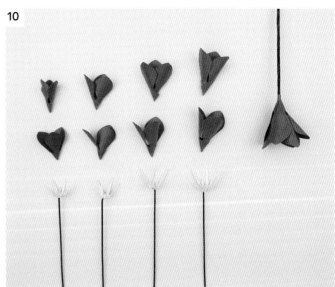

7. Pierce holes in the petal cones. First thread on the cone that has the tab glued on the outside. Next, thread on the petal cone that has the tab glued on the inside—this way all the tabs are hidden in the finished flower head.

8. Make sure the petal cones are offset from each other so that the inner petals sit between the outer petals. Glue the cones to each other.

9. Add glue to the underside of the flower center, then pull on the stem so that the center is pulled down and sits in the middle of the flower head.

10. Repeat steps 1–6 for each size of flower head.

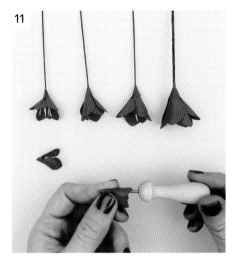

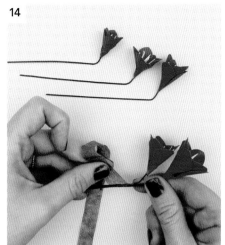

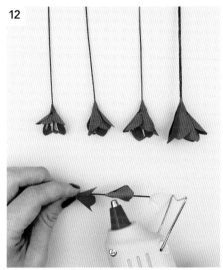

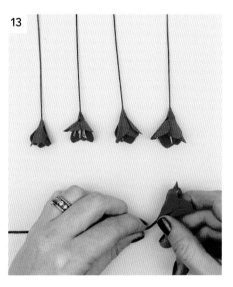

11. And then steps 7–9, piercing holes in the petal cones.

12. Glue the petal cone pairs to each other, pulling the centers into the middle of the flower heads.

13. Bend each stem to a 45-degree angle, around 0.5 in. (1 cm) from the base of the flower head.

14. Tape them in a row to the main stem, starting with the largest flower head at the very top.

15. Finish with the smallest.

16. Gently bend the main stem backward to form a realistic curve.

LILY OF THE VALLEY

Difficulty: Advanced
Base type: None!
Build type: Mini formed cones

These little bell-shaped flowers are particularly satisfying to make from paper—there is something infinitely pleasing about a flat sheet of paper being transformed into curvy blooms!

Thin or lightweight paper is the best choice for Lily of the Valley, as their size puts them at the fiddlier end of the blooming-paper scale. This is also why they have been classed as "advanced."

These flowers are famously pure white, but don't be afraid to stray from nature. Making flowers from colors that don't exist in reality is one of the big draws of this craft. For example, I've used a mustard-yellow version in the Bouquet project on page 124.

TOOLS AND MATERIALS

- ball tools—or round ended pencils
- bradawl or darning needle
- curling tool
- floristry tape
- floristry wire—1 long piece for the main stem, 5 shorter pieces for the flower stems
- foam mat or similar
- glue gun—optional
- needlenose pliers
- paper—offcuts for all components
- scissors, knife, or digital cutting machine
- tacky PVA glue (for beginners)

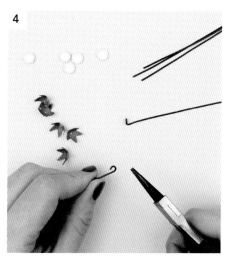

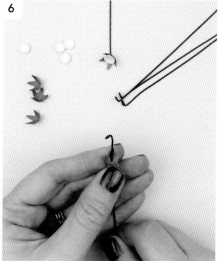

1. With a ball tool slightly narrower than the width of the disk, run the head around the small disks of card to form little domes.

2. Do the same with the star-shaped pieces.

3. Pierce a hole in the middle of the cupped star shapes.

4. With some pliers, bend a loop in the end of the short wires.

5. Then, bend the loop over so that it is at a 90-degree angle to the stem.

6. Slide the star shapes up toward the loop in the wire.

7. Add some glue over the wire loop, and sandwich it with one of the cupped disks. (A glue gun will give a more secure base, but it can be messy!)

8. Run a ball tool up each petal, from the middle of the strip to the rounded tips (see template for detail).

9. Tightly curl the pointed tips in the opposite direction to the last step.

10. Add glue to the tiny tab and roll the flower heads so that the curled, pointed petals (made in step 9) flick outward.

11. On the same side as the wire, add small blobs of glue to the points of the star. It's best to use glue that dries more slowly than a glue gun, to allow for some maneuverability in the next step.

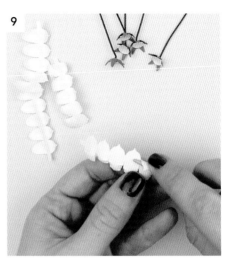

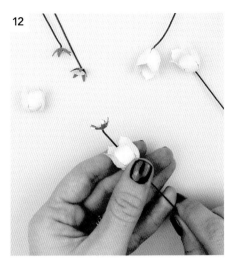

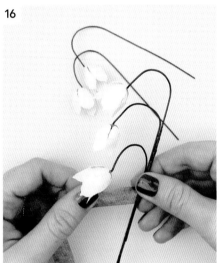

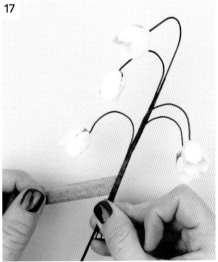

12. Thread the wire through the flower head from bottom to top, and glue the curved petal tops to the star piece, centering a petal on each star arm.

13. Once the flower heads are dried, gently bend the wire into an arch, as shown.

14. Start to wrap floristry tape midway down the first stem.

15. Add it to the end of the main wire stem.

16. Continue down the main stem, adding in the remaining flower heads as you go—

17. . . . until all of the wires are contained in tape.

DAHLIA

Difficulty: Average to advanced
Base type: Disk base
Build type: Layered

The dahlia is my favorite flower and also one of my favorites to make in paper. I love the graphic quality of a dahlia and the texture it brings to an arrangement or display.

There are a lot of petals to form, making this one of the more time-consuming blooms. However, once you have found your rhythm, it's pretty straightforward to make, and the finished flowers are always worth the extra time invested!

This is another flower that bridges the realistic/stylized aesthetic. I use it in the Bouquet project (see page 124), which focuses on more natural shapes, as well as in the Table Arrangement (see page 131), which is more stylized. You can also see them in my Window Display on page 138.

If you are hand-cutting this flower, a paper or thinner card is going to make your life easier, as it will allow you to cut on the fold for each layer (see page 21). However, if you have a particular heavier paper/card in mind, you can use the full template shape. For digital cutting machine users, a thicker material will give a sturdier bloom, whereas something more lightweight will give a softer effect.

TOOLS AND MATERIALS

- bradawl or darning needle
- curling tool
- disk base
- embossing tool—optional
- floristry tape
- floristry wire—1 long piece for the stem, 2 shorter pieces for the leaves

- glue—any type
- paper—as required for bases and leaves 1.5 A4 sheets for the petal layers
- scissors, knife, or digital cutting machine

1. Lay a straight curling tool down the center of each petal, and roll to bend them around the tool. Once the tool is removed, you might want to give them a little squeeze, too, to give a nice tight curve.

2. Curl the petals of the center strip.

3. Roll the center and glue the tab in place.

4. Curl the inner petal layers as shown.

5. If you have ball tools, run one around the middle of the inner petal layers. This step isn't essential; you could gently manipulate the pieces by hand instead.

6. Gather the three central components.

7. Glue the two inner petal layers on top of each other, offsetting them so that the petals from one fill the gaps between the petals of the other.

8. Add glue to the bottom edge of the rolled center.

9. Glue the center into the middle of the inner petals.

10. Gently fold up the petals of layers 4, 5, and 6. Glue them on top of each other, in size order—largest at the bottom, with the curl facing up. Remember to offset each layer as you go.

11. Glue the inner petals and the center into the middle of the three layers you have just constructed (petal layers 4, 5, and 6).

12. Order the remaining petal layers by size. Locate one layer 1 piece and gently fold the petals down—start with the petal curl facing up—the opposite way to step 10. This step makes sure there is space to fit all of the layers, plus it adds to the overall shape of the flower head.

13. Repeat—offset and glue the layers, starting with the largest at the bottom.

14. As you go, you'll find that you don't need to fold back the petals on all the layers—the dahlia form will naturally start to take shape.

15. Add the layered center into the middle of the main flower.

16. Glue the disk base to the underside of the flower.

17. Add the cone cover over the disk base.

18. Fold the leaves in half (prescoring is optional, but can be helpful).

19. Glue the ends of the short pieces of wire into the leaf, then pinch the paper around them to add shape.

20. Use floristry tape to attach the leaves to the stem.

ROSE

Difficulty: Advanced
Base type: Disk base—flat
Build type: Outward

The rose is a quintessentially English flower found in all kinds of floral design work in a glorious range of colors and varieties. The paper version of this flower is built up of simple shapes that are straightforward to cut out and form into petals. There are quite a few layers to the full rose, and some concentration is needed to get the correct placing, which is why it earns its advanced rating.

You can reduce the number of layers in this design, to replicate the different growth stages of a natural rose from bud to full bloom.

As far as paper is concerned, light weights to mid-weights are most suited, due to the number of petal layers in the full bloom.

The design of this flower means it suits projects where you are aiming for a more realistic feel. I used roses in the Bouquet (page 124) and a reduced bud version for the Buttonholes (page 120). There is also an extra large version in the Garland on page 128. This flower works brilliantly at a larger scale, and the individual petals can be as large as a sheet of paper each—giving a super-sized finished piece. When made at a larger scale, this flower takes on a more stylized aesthetic and is effective in all sorts of colors and finishes.

TOOLS AND MATERIALS

- bone folder—optional
- bradawl or darning needle
- curling tool
- disk base
- floristry tape

- floristry wire—1 x long piece for the stem, 1 x shorter piece for the leaf
- glue gun—optional
- paper—as required for bases and leaves 1.5 x A4 sheets for the petals
- PVA glue
- scissors, knife, or digital cutting machine

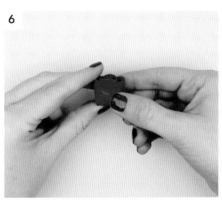

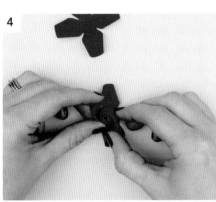

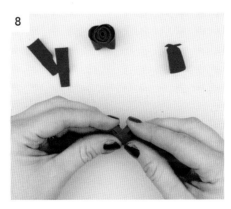

1. Curl the petals of the center layers inward at their corners.

2. Bend up two opposing petals and interlock as shown. Glue in place.

3. Repeat step 2 with the remaining opposing petals on this first layer.

4. Glue the first completed layer into the middle of the next center layer. Next, repeat the same steps on the opposing petals, gluing them to the first formed layer.

5. Glue the first two layers into the middle of the final center layer and repeat steps 2, 3, and 4 again.

6. The finished center layers form the base of the rose to which the individual petals are attached.

7. Curl petal 1 inward, vertically.

8. Cross the bottom tabs over to create the petal base and glue. The two resulting tabs (at right angles) provide a surface to apply glue for the next step. (this photo shows the petal viewed from the bottom).

9. Turn the central base section over. Apply glue to the tabs on the petals, and glue the first layer of individual petals on the bottom of the base section, matching the corners of the center piece with the right angles of the petals. Each petal will overlap the previous one slightly.

10. Before gluing the fourth petal on, slip the edge of the petal underneath the first that you stuck down. Follow the photo guide.

11. Top view of the result of steps 1–10.

12. Repeat the same petal curling and forming methods as for petal 1, with the four petal 2 pieces, but overlap the tabs at 45 degrees—rather than 90 degrees.

13. Hold the petal tabs and curl the corners of these petals outward—so in the opposite direction to the initial curl.

14. Turn the rose over again and add the next layer of petals. This time, add them to the sides of the square base rather than to the corners, so that the layers are offset and the petals sit in between those in the first layer.

15. Repeat the petal forming process (steps 13–14) with the four petal 3s. Add them to the rose so that the petals overlap the join between the petals on the previous layer.

16. The final two layers of petals are formed slightly differently. First, place a straight tool down the length of the petal and bend it around the tool.

17. Then, curl the corners of the petals outward—in the opposite direction to the bend.

18. Overlap the petal tabs and glue.

19. Add the petal 4's to the rest of the rose. Again, they should be offset, centered over the join between the petals on the previous layer.

20. Add the stem base on the underside of the rose.

21. The final layer of petals is glued over the disk of the stem base.

22. Curl the leaves on the cone cover.

23. Then glue it to the underside of the rose.

24. Apply glue to one of the leaf shapes, and add the short wire stem.

25. Place the other leaf shape on top and flatten it down, so that the wire is securely sandwiched.

26. Attach the leaf to the main stem with floristry wire.

To create a more budlike rose, simply stop at step 14, then add the base and cone cover.

GARDEN ROSE

Difficulty: Very advanced
Base type: Disk base
Build type: Outward

This is the most advanced flower in the book, but it still features the same basic techniques as other flowers. You can see the design process for this flower on page 40.

I see a lot of garden roses in fresh bridal bouquets, and, like their fresh counterparts, these paper blooms add a lovely texture to floral designs with their intricate, layered petals.

Like the Ranunculus and standard Rose, this flower is built from the center, working outward with a disk base, layered between petals. Any paper (or very thin card) will work for this bloom. Experiment with different weights to see which works best for you.

I used this flower for the Bouquet project (see page 124) as I wanted a more realistic look with a summer bride in mind.

TOOLS AND MATERIALS

- bradawl or darning needle
- curling tool
- disk base
- floristry tape
- floristry wire
- glue—any type
- paper—as required for bases;
  1 A4 sheet for the petals
- scissors, knife, or digital cutting machine
- small clothespins—optional

1. Tightly roll petal 1—

2. . . . around a thin curling tool.

3. Add a small amount of glue onto one edge and overlap the other edge, gluing the petals into small cylinders. Small clothespins are handy to hold these together while they dry.

4. Roll the next two sizes of petals (petals 2 and 3) but don't glue them.

5. Overlap the tabs on all three sizes to form the petals.

6. The smallest petals have a very short cut and, therefore, a steep overlap.

7. Add a small amount of glue to the closed tip of petal 1, stick it inside petal 2, and then glue both into petal 3. Repeat until you have four sets of nesting petals.

8. Curl the center strip.

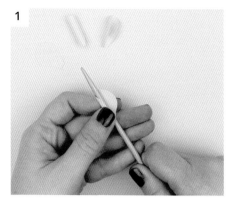

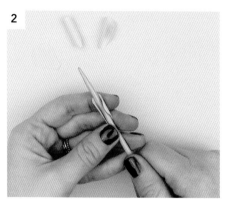

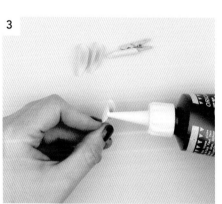

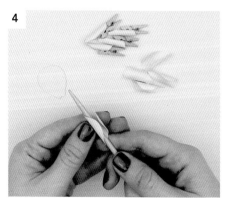

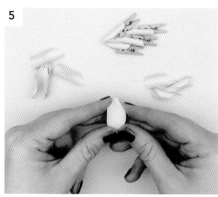

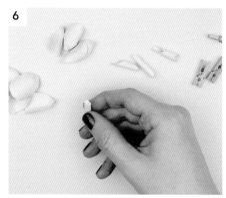

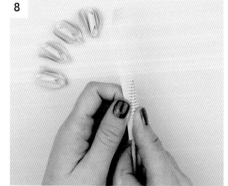

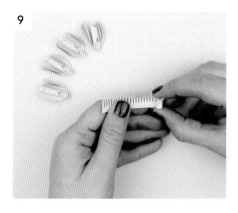

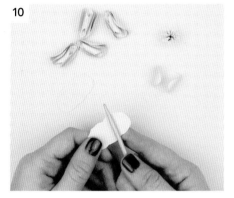

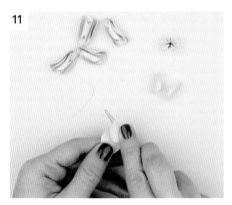

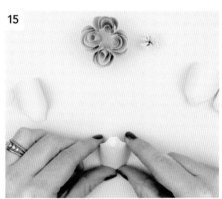

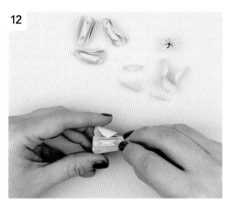

9. Roll the center strip so that the curl is directed outward, and secure the end with glue.

10. Hold your curling tool from the dip to the point on petal 4 (see the template for detail)—

11. . . . and curl it inward.

12. Glue the petal nests from steps 1–7 into petal 4.

13. Glue the nested petals to each other, at right angles.

14. Curl petal 5 inward, vertically.

15. Overlap and glue the tabs to form the petals.

16. Glue the first petal onto the disk base.

17. Repeat with all four petals so that they interlock as shown—the right-hand edge of each petal sits over the left-hand edge of the one next to it.

18. Add glue to the tips of the nested petal sets.

19. Glue the central petals into the first layer of the main petals; the inner petals should sit in the overlapped joins of the petals in the underlayer.

20. Glue the curled and rolled center into the middle of the flower.

21. Repeat the same petal formation (as already made for petal 5) for petals 6–8.

22. Turn the rose over and add the next petal layer on the underside.

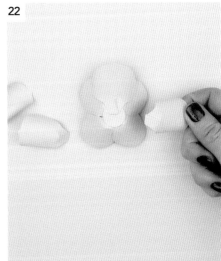

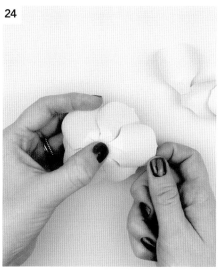

23. Offset the petals so that the petals in the latest layer sit over the overlaps between the petals in the underlying previous layer.

24. Repeat with the next size of petals.

25. Add the stem base in, before the final layer of petals.

26. The last layer of petals is formed in the same way as the previous layers, but the top edge is also pinched in the middle.

27. Add these to the flower, in the same way as the previous layers now covering the stem base.

28. Push the cone cover up the stem, toward the flower. Glue into place.

WILLOW EUCALYPTUS

This foliage uses a single stem and a set of leaves in graduating sizes. The leaves are bent and pinched around the main stem, from smallest at the top to largest at the bottom. I have used a simple pointed shape, but of course you can use any shape of leaf you choose.

Any thickness of card or paper works well for leaves on this type of stem. The only thing to really consider is the glue you use—if you're using a thicker medium, a glue gun works best.

Leaves create a graphic feel that adds shape and texture to arrangements. I have used this foliage in the cover photograph and for the Table Arrangement (page 131), as well as the Wreath (page 106), and in the Bouquet (page 124).

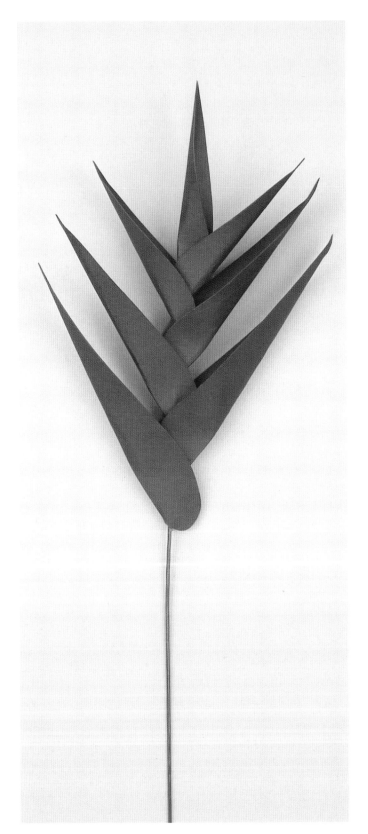

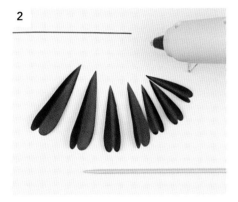

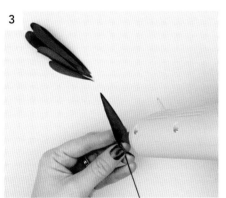

1. Bend the leaves around a straight tool.

2. Repeat for all leaf sizes.

3. Start with the smallest leaf. Hold the floristry wire stem at the bottom center of the leaf, and add glue to the curved section.

4. Pinch the two curved sections together, around the wire stem.

5. Repeat steps 3–4 for the next leaf, attaching it at an angle.

6. Carry on down the stem, increasing the leaf size as you go.

7. The finished foliage

MAGNOLIA LEAVES

The leaves in this stem become textured after forming. They are created using a simple fold and concertina, and the result is highly effective. As the finished leaves are quite large, I prefer to use one leaf per stem so that they can be evenly distributed throughout an arrangement. The leaves are attached to the stems with a pinch—similar to the way that the Willow Eucalyptus leaves are attached.

Thinner or lighter-weight papers work best for this leaf, as there is a lot of folding through double layers. I have used a lovely textured paper here (I also used it for the Bouquet project—see page 124). Additionally, I made a gold version for the Table Arrangement piece (page 131).

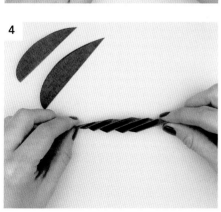

1. Fold the leaves in half, lengthways (pre-scoring is optional).

2. Hold the leaf at a 45-degree angle on a flat surface, with the fold toward you. Fold down about a quarter of an inch (0.5 cm) at the top, parallel to you.

3. Continue to concertina the leaf, keeping the folds parallel to the first fold.

4. The fully concertina-folded leaf

5. Gently open the leaf up.

6. Add glue to the bottom of the leaf and pinch it around a piece of floristry wire.

7. Mix different leaf sizes to add texture to your displays.

MEADOW FLOWER FOLIAGE

This foliage was inspired by the image that I reference in the "Designs to Inspire" chapter on page 38. I traced the leaf shapes from a vintage botanical illustration.

The result was one main stem with a series of individual stems that are attached to it. You will need one long main wire and then between two and eight shorter pieces, depending on how many more leaves you want to add to the stem. As with the previous two construction methods, try different leaf shapes to get a wide range of effects. Remember that each individual leaf is made up of a pair of shapes. So cut out twice as many finished leaves as you want.

I used this foliage in the Bouquet project (page 124). The way that the stems are built brings a more natural softness that worked well in this arrangement.

1

4

2

5

3

1. Add glue to one in a pair of leaf shapes.

2. Place and glue the other leaf in the pair on top of the first, sandwiching the main wire stem in between the layers.

3. Curl the leaf slightly before the glue completely dries.

4. Repeat steps 1–3 with all the leaf sizes, adding the shorter pieces of wire to the relevant-sized leaves.

5. Add the leaves with shorter stems to the main wire stem.

BABY BLUE EUCALYPTUS

This foliage is inspired by natural baby blue eucalyptus—a firm favorite with florists. The stem has a unique shape: a row of evenly spaced leaves stacked on top of each other.

This final foliage stem uses another construction method: double leaf shapes are curled and then threaded onto one central wire stem. Varying the direction of the leaf curls adds interest to floral designs. I used thin drinking straws to space the leaves apart from each other; alternatively, you could create your own narrow tubes of paper.

I used this stem in a realistic green color in the Bouquet project (page 124) and in a pearlized gold in the Table Arrangement (page 131).

1. Cover three drinking straws with floristry tape.

2. Cut two of the straws into pieces that are approximately 0.5 in. (1.5 cm) long.

3. Thread the floristry wire through the full straw and bend the end back on itself, up the outside of the straw.

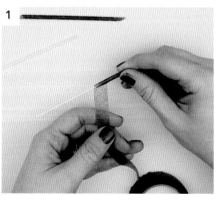

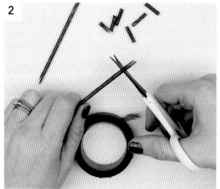

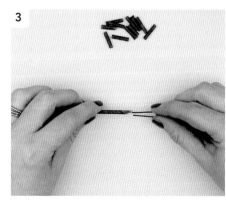

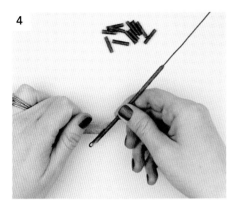

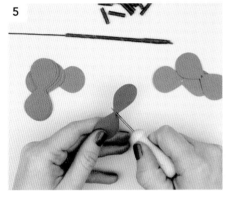

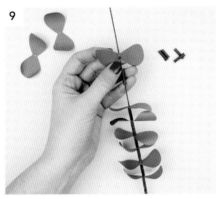

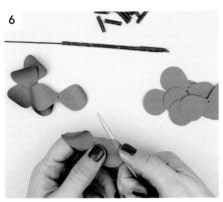

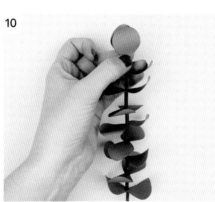

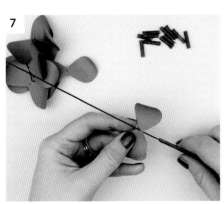

4. With floristry tape, wrap together the bent wire end and the straw to secure them.

5. Pierce holes in the middle of all the leaf shapes.

6. Curl the leaves in random directions and at random angles.

7. Thread the first leaf onto the wire right down to the drinking straw.

8. Slide on one of the short pieces of straw.

9. Repeat steps 7–8 until you reach the end of the wire stem.

10. Thread the last leaf onto the tip of the wire. Add some glue and pinch the leaf around the wire.

11. Gently pinch each leaf up around the stem.

PROJECTS
TO MAKE

WREATH

Time: ● ● ●
Skill: ● ●

Wreaths can be adapted to suit all seasons and make great wall décor as well as being used on doors. You could also make double-sided versions and hang them at a celebration or in a window display where they would spin.

This project is a good example of using flower heads with no stems, alongside stemmed foliage. You can use any of the flowers in this book for this project: just select the most suitable of the suggested attaching methods for your chosen blooms.

I have chosen a jewel-toned pallette that is set off well by this front door. Think carefully about where the wreath will be placed when you are choosing your colors and papers. If you're placing it somewhere outdoors, choose a sheltered spot and add a waterproof finish to the flowers to give some level of weatherproofing.

I have designed one large feature flower for this project—loosely inspired by a sunflower. It is constructed in much the same way as the Daisy but on a much larger scale. You could also add a stem base and cone cover to this flower and use it in other projects, such as in the Table Arrangement (page 131) or Bouquet (see page 124).

A variety of layouts would work well if you were making a series or set of wreaths: make some symmetrical, some asymmetric; some full, some minimal.

The base for the wreath utilizes the outer ring of the embroidery hoop used for the Chandelier project (see page 113).

YOU WILL NEED

- curling tools
- floristry tape
- floristry wire
- glue
- needle-nose pliers
- outer section of a 12 in. (30 cm) embroidery hoop
- scissors, knife, or digital cutting machine

PAPER QUANTITIES

For these examples, I used
- aqua—2 A4 sheets
- dark green—leftover pieces
- gold— leftover pieces
- pink—2 A4 sheets
- purple—2 A4 sheets
- silver—1 A4 sheet
- teal— leftover pieces
- turquoise—half A4 sheet

1. Construct the sunflower: lay a straight curling tool down the center of each petal and bend them around the tool.

2. Glue the petal layers together, offsetting them from each other.

3. Gently bend the petals upward to give the flower more fullness.

4. Bend the petals in the first layer of the center, in the same way as the main petals.

5. Fold the petals of center layer 1 upward.

6. Curl the petals on the center pieces (2–5).

7. Curl the sunflower center strips in the same way as a daisy center is prepared.

8. Roll the center strips so that the curl is directed inward (opposite to a daisy's center).

9. Add the next two strips around the first.

10. Add the center layers to the flower, offsetting the petals as you go.

11. Finish with the rolled center strips.

12. Score and fold all of the large leaves.

13. Score and fold the small triple-pointed leaves as per templates. Note that the white dotted line indicates mountain folds, and the black dotted line indicates valley folds (see "Techniques to Study," page 14).

14. Curl the tips of the anemone leaves, away from the valley fold.

15. Curl and roll the mini peony and bud centers (refer to standard Peony instructions on page 53 if needed).

16. Curl and form the bud petals (following instructions in "Flowers and Foliage to Master" on page 44) and add the centers.

17. Fold up the petals on the mini peony center, and layer it in alongwith the vertical fringe.

18. Construct the Peonies, Daisies, Buttercups, and Willow Eucalyptus stems as per the instructions in the early chapters of this book. Lay out the components, ready for attaching to the embroidery hoop.

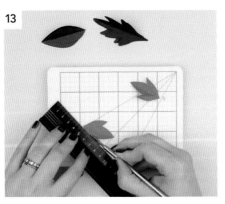

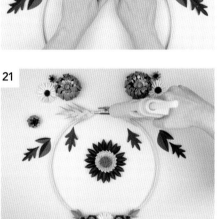

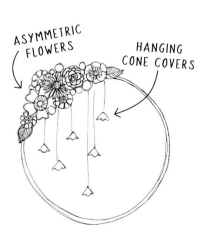

19. Make sure the tightening screw is at the top; it usefully provides a hanging point for the finished wreath. Glue the bottom set of flowers to the hoop and join the two foliage stems to each other with floristry tape. (You can add any stemmed flowers you want to the hoop by using floristry tape.)

20. Glue the foliage stems centrally across the top of the embroidery hoop. (You could alternatively attach stems to the hoop with floristry tape.)

21. Add glue to the middle for the Sunflower head.

22. Work around the hoop, adding first the leaves, then layering the flowers on top.

23. Finish with the mini Peonies and Peony Buds.

ALTERNATIVE LAYOUTS

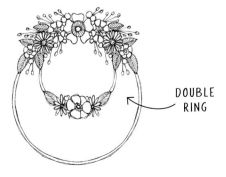

FULL FLORAL

ASYMMETRIC FLOWERS

HANGING CONE COVERS

DOUBLE RING

CAKE TOPPER

Time: ● ●
Skill: ● ●

This is another project that is very easy to adapt to suit your celebration or occasion. I have used a playful color pallette and the number 4 with a child's birthday in mind. You could, as an example, use the color pallette from the table arrangement and replace the 4 with the initials of a couple who are celebrating their wedding. Or make it all in one color for a more sophisticated celebration, such as an adult's important birthday. Take a look at the Window Display on page 138. This uses monochromatic flowers and might give you some ideas to use.

I have made the flower heads without stems so that they are flatbacked. For this reason I chose the Daisy, Buttercup, and Meadow Flower, as they are all constructed using either a flat base or horizontal layers, rather than a cone base.

The cake shown here is a three-tier, 9 in. (23 cm) cake. You may want to increase or decrease the size of the flowers you use if your cake is a very different size to this.

Think about color, and the overall shape and balance when you are designing your own topper. I have gone for an asymmetric layout for this example, but something more symmetrical would work just as well. I have also made some little cupcake decorations in coordinating colors, using the Billy Buttons flower design.

YOU WILL NEED
- curling tool, fine rounded
- glue—any type
- quilling tool—optional
- scissors, knife, or digital cutting machine
- wooden skewers (4)

PAPER QUANTITIES
For these examples, I used
- gold—1 A4 sheet
- mint—half A4 sheet
- neon pink—1 A4 sheet
- pale pink—1 A4 sheet
- teal—half A4 sheet

1. Make the two Daisies following the instructions in "Flowers and Foliage to Master" on page 56.

2. The Meadow Flower instructions are on page 38.

3. Instructions for the Buttercup can be found in "Blooms to Practice" on page 34.

4. Arrange the three non-floral cake topper components in the correct configuration on a flat surface. Then lay the wooden skewers on top to get the correct placement and spacing.

5. Glue the skewer to the disk and add glue to the reverse of the branch.

6. Place the disk of the branch piece over the disk on the skewer, and sandwich the skewer between the two.

7. Repeat this with your chosen numeral. I have also added in shorter sections of skewer around the 4, so that the two layers are evenly spaced.

8. Repeat with the second branch.

9. Add the flowers to the branches in the layout shown.

ALTERNATIVE LAYOUTS

CHANDELIER

Time: • • • • •
Skill: • •

This is a delightfully playful design that works well in the home, at a special event, or even in a retail display. As with the other projects, simply altering the color pallette can make it suitable for all sorts of seasons and occasions.

For the Chandelier, paper flowers and leaves are glued to an embroidery hoop, and paper emulates ribbon—though, of course, you can replace these with actual ribbons.

I have used some of the flowers in different sizes from those described in the techniques and practice flower chapters. Templates for these and the ribbons can be found at the back of this book.

The design is loosely inspired by Polish Pajaki, which traditionally feature paper pom-poms and beads in bright colors. The bottom of each drop of my Chandelier features a pom-pom that's built in the same way as the Billy Buttons flowers. Also, rather than using the usual flower center, I have added a layered Peony Bud and long-fringed vertical center to give a tassel shape.

I have chosen to use more stylized, graphic flowers to add to the fun aesthetic of the finished piece. As with the Cake Topper, there are no stems—only the flower heads are used. For this reason, I have used flowers that have flat backs rather than cone bases, although cone base flowers would work well at the end of the paper ribbons.

The flowers in this design are all simple, but—there are a lot of them! It will aid construction if you prep all the flower heads before making the Chandelier itself. I also recommend reading the instructions through from start to finish before you begin.

For the hoop I used a 12 in. (30 cm) wooden embroidery ring. If you have a smaller or larger hoop, be mindful that the swagged ribbons will need adjusting accordingly to fill the hoop evenly.

YOU WILL NEED
- curling tools
- embossing tool—optional
- glue—any type
- inner ring of a 12 in. (30 cm) embroidery hoop
- ruler—optional
- scissors, knife, or digital cutting machine

PAPER QUANTITIES
For these examples, I used:
- coral red—3 A4 sheets
- lilac—2 A4 sheet
- orange—2 A4 sheets
- pink—3 A4 sheets
- teal—2 A4 sheet
- turquoise—2 A4 sheet
- yellow—5 A4 sheets

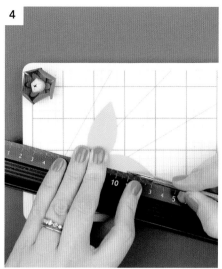

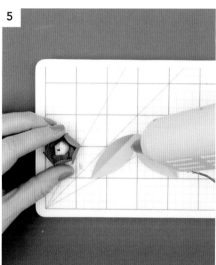

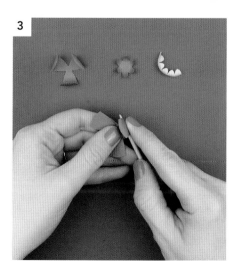

1. Score the large leaves, using the dashed lines on the template as a guide.

2. Fold the leaves, referring to the templates. The white dotted lines are mountain folds, and the black dotted lines are valley folds. (See "Techniques to Study," page 14.)

3. Make the Buttercup following the instructions on page 34.

4. Score and (valley) fold the double leaves.

5. Glue the red buttercups onto the double leaves.

6. Swag 1: Glue the double leaves to the bottom/middle of the swag. Repeat five times.

7. Swag 2: Make five mini peonies—a vertical, outward center, and petal layers following the Peony Bud instructions in page 44. Note that the petal layer is a different shape for this project. Glue the mini peony in the middle of swag 2 and add two of the orange Buttercups either side. Repeat five times.

8. Glue the tops of swag 1 to swag 2, then repeat so that you have five pairs.

9. Construct five Camellia heads, following the instructions on page 28.

10. The tassel pom-poms: Curl two of the tassel outer shapes as shown, and construct the tassel inner as you would a vertical/outward flower center (refer to "Techniques to Study" on page 25). The pom-pom part is the same as a Billy Button but without the layered fringed center.

11. Glue the tassel inner into the outer.

12. Add this to the pom-pom.

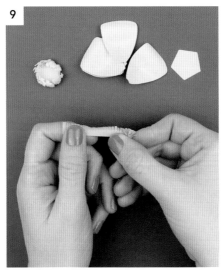

13. Gather one of each of the flowers shown (you also need five Meadow Flowers and five Daisies for this project, as detailed in the templates). Fold the ribbon 0.5 in. (1 cm) from the end, across its width, as shown.

14. Then, fold it back in the opposite direction a small fraction of an inch (about 0.5 cm)—see photo 14 opposite.

15. Add glue to the middle section.

16. Glue the folded end down so that you end up with a tab, as shown.

17. This tab provides the base to be glued into the pom-pom.

18. Glue the Meadow Flower at the other end of the ribbon.

19. Glue the Camellia below the Meadow Flower and add the Daisy below the Camellia.

20. Add the hanging loop onto the top web center by threading it through the slit, then gluing the end tabs down on the reverse. Now, glue the arms to the center.

21. Glue the small leaves over the joins on the underside (opposite side from the hanging loop).

22. Construct the small Peony, following the instructions on page 53, but do not add a stem. Glue the flower into the middle of the leaves.

23. The "bottom web" is constructed in the same way as the top (see step 19).

24. Glue the medium Peony into the middle, turn it over, and add the medium leaves, as shown.

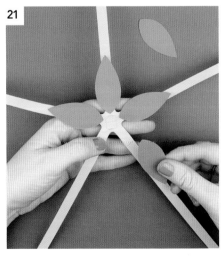

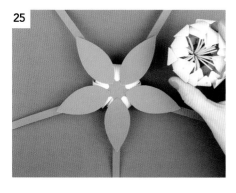

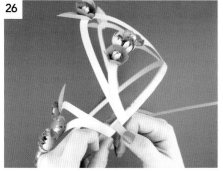

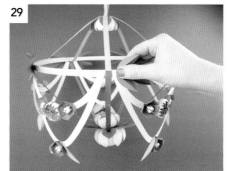

25. Glue the standard size Peony into the middle of the leaves.

26. Glue one swag pair to your embroidery hoop, then one end of one arm of the "top web" before you add the next swag. Repeat this all the way around the embroidery hoop.

27. This sets the spacing for the rest of the chandelier components. Hanging the chandelier at this stage will greatly aid the remaining construction steps, and help you keep the spacing and balance correct.

28. Add the hoop cover strips to the sections of embroidery hoop between the swags.

29. Glue on the large leaves in pairs.

30. Glue the Meadow Flower drops prepared in steps 9–18 into the middle of the large leaf pairs.

ALTERNATIVE IDEA
Add floral drops and swags to a straight pole to make a wall hanging, or even use it as a ceremonial backdrop.

BUTTONHOLES

Time: ● ● ●
Skill: ● ● ●

Buttonholes—or *boutonnieres*—are a traditional wedding corsage, but don't be put off if that isn't relevant to you. These mini arrangements are very versatile. You could add one to a special wrapped gift or embellish a photo frame with one, or even two.

I have strayed from a natural color pallette for this project by adding in some pale aqua highlights and bronze mini leaves. Color pallette inspiration can come from anywhere—look at nature or graphic design (e.g., packaging and magazines)— because the colors featured will have been carefully considered to complement each other.

I've chosen to use a mix of styles with realistic flowers and stylized filler flowers and foliage. Using more unusual colors often pulls the two styles together. The little cone fillers that I used here also feature in my Table Arrangement (page 131) and are a great way to add a pop of color to designs.

I've chosen to make three different designs that complement each other rather than match exactly: I like to think of the individuals who will wear them for the special day, and make their buttonholes to reflect and complement them.

YOU WILL NEED
- double-sided tape
- floristry tape
- floristry wire
- glue gun—optional
- needlenose pliers—optional
- PVA glue
- range of curling tools
- scissors, knife, or digital cutting machine

PAPER QUANTITIES
For these examples, I used
- aqua—1 A4 sheet
- blush—1 A4 sheet
- bright yellow—half A4 sheet
- bronze—1 A4 sheet
- mustard—1 A4 sheet
- pale yellow—1 A4 sheet
- rust—1 A4 sheet

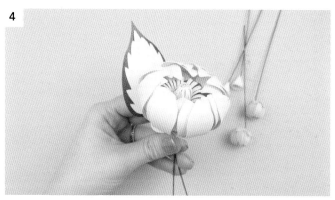

1. Make all flowers following the instructions in the "Flowers and Foliage to Master" chapter, starting on page 43.

2. Buttonholes numbers 1 and 3 feature small cone fillers. With needle-nose pliers (or by hand if you don't have pliers), curl the shape around on itself.

3. Slot the end of a length of floristry wire into the cone and glue down the end of the paper, over the wire.

4. To make the first buttonhole, hold together the Peony and a large leaf.

5. Slot the Peony Buds in between the flower and the leaf.

6

9

7

10

8

11

6. Add in the mini cone fillers and secure the stems with floristry tape.

7. Run the double-sided tape down the paper ribbon strip (you can also use glue here if you don't have double-sided tape).

8. Wrap the stems with the "ribbon" (a strip of paper in coordinating colors).

9. Glue a piece of the strip around the top of the wrapped ribbon to hide the join. Trim the ends.

10. The next two buttonhole examples feature some mini leaf stems. Bend each leaf on the stem around a straight curling tool.

11. Again, construct all the other flowers following the "Flowers and Foliage to Master" chapter instructions.

12. Gather the stems.

13. Finish by adding the mini leaf stems at the back of the grouping and repeat steps 6–9 to secure the stems.

14. Finally, for the third design, construct all the flowers following "Flowers and Foliage to Master" instructions.

15. Group them together and fasten in the same way again.

ALTERNATIVE USES

If these are being made for a wedding, it's a nice touch to use the same stems to make flower crowns and larger posies for the bridesmaids. These posies are basically mini arrangements that can also be used for all sorts of non-wedding related decorations, such as some extra-special gift wrapping.

BOUQUET

Time: ●●●●
Skill: ●●●

It would be remiss to write a book about flowers and not include a bouquet! A paper flower bouquet can be a great alternative to a fresh one for lots of reasons. Perhaps your favorite flower is out of season: then make it! Or, you're getting married, but are allergic to fresh flowers. Maybe you have an unusual color scheme in mind that can't be replicated with natural flowers. Or you could be looking for a gift for a first anniversary, where paper is traditionally given. Or, you would simply like some paper blooms in your home.

For this bouquet, I have imagined a spring or summer wedding themed with pretty pastels. I chose to concentrate on the more realistic flowers from my collection, but you could, of course, substitute them for others that you prefer or enjoy making. The key is to mix not only colors and tones, but also textures. You can achieve a good mix of texture by using different-sized flowers or flowers of different shapes, and by adding in plenty of foliage. I have used a Lily of the Valley in mustard as the filler flowers—they add pops of bold color and help create the loose, hand-tied feel of the arrangement.

These instructions focus on how to arrange and tie a bouquet, so refer back to the "Flowers and Foliage to Master" (starting on page 43) for the instructions for individual flowers. All the flowers in this book are suitable for a bouquet.

YOU WILL NEED

- floristry tape
- floristry wire
- glue—any type
- knife or digital cutting machine
- pliers
- range of curling tools
- ribbon—3 ft. (1 m)
- scissors
- wire cutters

FLOWERS AND FOLIAGE

You can use any flower(s) for an arrangement like this. However, this example bouquet uses

- 2 Cream Garden Roses
- 3 Lemon Tulips
- 3 Lilac Anemones
- 6 Magnolia leaves
- 3 Meadow Flower foliage stems
- 4 Mustard Lily of the Valley stems
- 3 Pink Freesia stems
- 3 Pink Roses
- 3 Purple Ranunculuses
- 5 White Daisies
- 5 Willow Eucalyptus stems

PAPER QUANTITIES

For this example, I used

- beige—2 A4 sheets
- lilac—2 A4 sheets
- mustard—1 A4 sheets
- off white—4 A4 sheets
- pale yellow—2 A4 sheets
- pink—4 A4 sheets
- various greens—10 A4 sheets
- white—1 A4 sheet

1. Hold one large and two medium flowers in a bunch. I used one Rose, one Anemone, and one Tulip.

2. Layer in some foliage and more flowers. To get an even base of different colors and textures, I used a Garden Rose and a Ranunculus.

3. Continue to layer in more foliage and flowers, roughly keeping a round shape at the core.

4. Start to consider the overall shape of the final bouquet: I added in two Freesia stems and some more foliage.

5. Continue layering in the rest of your larger flowers, taking a step back to ensure even, round coverage.

6. Add in your filler flowers. I used yellow Lily of the Valley.

7. Once you are happy with the overall shape of your bouquet, wrap the stems together with floristry tape. Pick out one of the colors to use for the ribbon.

8. Tie the ribbon around the taped section.

1

2

3

4

5

6

7

8

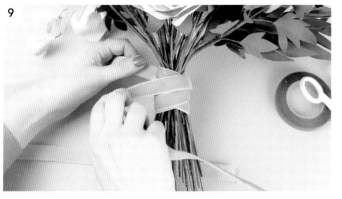

9. Wrap the stems with the ribbon.

10. Tie the ribbon off.

11. Finish with a bow.

12. Trim the flower stems to an even length.

WATERFALL BOUQUET

SMALL POSEY

ALTERNATIVE BOUQUET SHAPES

I find these hand-tied bouquets really inspiring. You could also try a waterfall arrangement, or perhaps a small posy that could be tied to a chair on a wedding aisle, or given as a house-warming gift.

GARLAND

Time: ● ● ● ●
Skill: ● ● ●

A simple design that uses oversized versions of the flowers. The flowers are attached in graduating size, and I have used an ombre color pallette to accentuate the overall shape.

This piece could be hung up in your home on a wall: it would also make a great celebration decoration— or it could be doubled up to dress a mantelpiece or even used as a decorative table runner.

This project demonstrates supersizing the flowers. You will need to upsize the templates at the back of the book or download the templates from the publisher's website. If you are upsizing, these are the flowers and dimensions you will need:

Rose—240%
Anemone—215%
Peony—190% (apart from the petal layer, a larger version of which is in two halves on pages 165–166)
Daisy—195%
Meadow Flower—100%

You can supersize any of the flowers in this book, simply by enlarging the templates on a photocopier or scanner, or by taking a photo and printing out the enlarged shapes.

I am usually drawn to papers for their color and finish and don't pay so much attention to their weight or thickness. However, if you are making very large flowers, it is a good idea to use slightly heavier stock, to ensure the stability of the finished flowers. Be prepared to play and experiment with papers and techniques.

YOU WILL NEED
- curling tools, including one large one
- embossing tool—optional
- glue—any type
- knife or digital cutting machine
- ruler—optional
- scissors

PAPER QUANTITIES
For this example, I used five shades of blue paper:
- blue (1)—3 A4 sheets
- blue (2)—7 A4 sheets
- blue (3)—3 A4 sheets
- blue (4)—2 A4 sheets
- darkest blue (5)—8 A4 sheets
- white —2 A4 sheets

1. Add glue to the tab on giant peony petal layer 1, and attach the two petal layers together.

2. Continue to make the peony, following the instructions on page 53.

3. All the other flowers are also made in exactly the same way as described in the "Flowers and Foliage to Master" chapter—except bigger! Gather the finished flowers.

4. Score the leaves lengthways.

5. Fold the leaves in half.

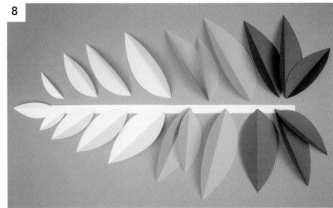

6. Cut two 1 in. (2 cm) wide strips from the long edge of an A4 piece of paper and glue them together.

7. Lay the leaves out as shown.

8. Glue all the leaves to the paper strip, one side at a time.

9. Work your way down the garland, gluing the flowers as you go. Flower order: Rose, Anemone, Peony, Daisy, and, finally, Meadow Flower.

ALTERNATIVE LAYOUTS

This garland would work well doubled up and added to a mantelpiece or used as a decorative table runner. Adding a loop of wire or cord to the back of larger flowers makes them suitable for hanging on a wall.

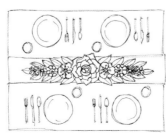

EXTRA LEAVES

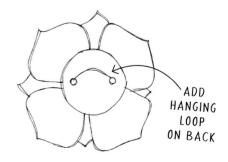

ADD HANGING LOOP ON BACK

TABLE ARRANGEMENT

Time: ●●●●●
Skill: ●●●●

Table arrangements are a simple way to add a statement focal point to an event or interior. By making your own from paper, you can reuse it again and again.

I chose to make this arrangement in a neutral pallette so that it would look equally at home on a festive table, as it would on my mantelpiece all year round. The flowers are all tones of white, gray, and taupe, whereas the foliage and highlight fillers are in a range of metallic golds. When using one color tone, add interest to your display by using a mix of paper textures and finishes. For example, I have used a velum for the Carnations, a pearlescent finish for the Dahlia, and matt, textured paper for the Peonies.

The display features a lot of flowers for extra drama, but you can, of course, adapt the arrangement for your own interior space by using a smaller vase and fewer flowers. Or, a larger vase and even more blooms! In this project there are some bonus flowers that haven't been featured elsewhere in the book, so the instructions start with how to make those.

It's a good idea to carefully consider your vase and make sure it is suitable for your intended design. This vintage brass pedestal vase is perfect for this particular project, as the brass finish goes well with my theme, and the metal grid (flower frog) makes arranging the flowers really easy. I have added gravel to the vase to give the arrangement some extra stability: this is also more eco-friendly than traditional flower foam.

This project focuses on how to arrange flowers for a table; please refer back to the "Flowers and Foliage to Master" chapter from page 43 for individual flower construction.

YOU WILL NEED

- curling tools
- drinking straws (for the Eucalyptus)
- floristry tape
- floristry wire
- needle-nose pliers—optional
- scissors, knife, or digital cutting machine
- wire cutters

FLOWERS

You can use any flower or flowers for an arrangement like this. This example uses:
- 6 Baby Blue Eucalyptus
- 6 Billy Buttons
- 5 Buttercups
- 3 Carnations
- 3 Cone Sprays (see instructions, page 133)
- 2 Daffodils
- 3 Dahlia
- 3 Fringed Daisies (see instructions, page 133)
- 3 Fritillarias
- 3 Large Peonies (additional templates, page 165)
- 12 Magnolia leaves
- 4 Meadow Flowers
- 4 Peonies
- 12 Peony Buds
- 6 Willow Eucalyptus

PAPER QUANTITIES

For these examples, I used
- golds—10 A4 sheets
- whites/neutrals—20 A4 sheets

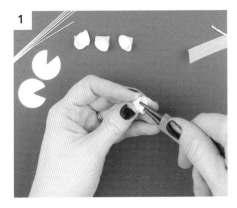

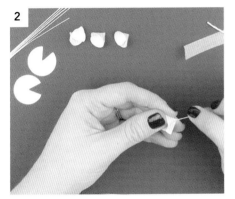

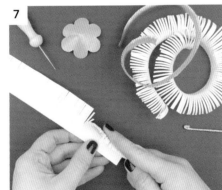

CONE SPRAY

1. With needlenose pliers (or by hand if you don't have pliers), curl the shape around on itself.

2. Slot the end of a length of floristry wire into the cone. Now glue down the end of the paper, over the wire.

3. Repeat steps 1 and 2, four to six times. Gather the stems together and wrap them in floristry tape.

4. Add to a wire stem and continue to wrap.

5. Continue down the main stem until all the shorter stems are enclosed in tape.

6. Gently ease the individual stems apart.

FRINGE DAISY

7. Curl all four fringed strips.

8. Roll the narrowest strip around a stem so that the curls are directed outward.

9. Manipulate the center with your fingers.

10. Wrap the center with the fringed strips, gluing as you go.

11. Construct a cone cover (page 19).

12. Fold up the cone's leaves, as shown.

13. Slide the cone up the stem.

14. Glue the cone leaves to the side of the rolled flower head.

ARRANGING THE FLOWERS

15. Add gravel to the bottom of the vase to stabilize it and gather together your flowers and foliage.

16. Mark the height of the finished arrangement with some tall foliage stems.

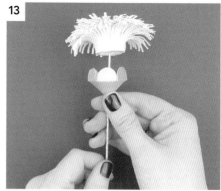

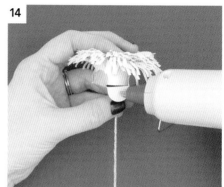

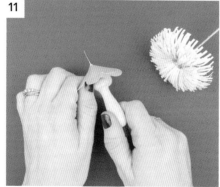

17. Add in different foliage for texture.

18. Continue to layer in base foliage to set the overall shape of the arrangement.

19. Add in several larger base flowers: trim the stems as you go to get the correct heights in the arrangement.

20. Layer in more flowers.

21. Continue adding flowers. Remember to take a step back from time to time to assess your arrangement as you go.

22. Add in your highlight filler flowers and fill in any other spaces.

ALTERNATIVE IDEA AND DIY PEDESTAL VASE

Glass bottles filled with paper flowers give a more informal aesthetic. You could also make you own dramatic pedestal vase by upcycling an inexpensive candlestick, pot, or dish.

INSTALLATIONS

This final chapter features three larger-scale installations. Each one utilizes paper flowers in a different way.

The first is a Window Display that uses a single color for the flowers to create a graphic backdrop to one giant feature dahlia. Next, a dramatic hanging Floral Cloud is created by using a mixture of flower styles. And finally, a mid-century inspired Wedding Arch with oversized blooms and hanging foliage.

I will take you behind the scenes to get a peak at what goes into designing, planning, and manufacturing large-scale commercial commissions.

WINDOW DISPLAY

The Cake Room in Hastings has a distinct identity, which is reflected in the interior design. The venue is known for its excellent cake and coffee, its extensive houseplant collection, bare brick walls teamed with copper pipe detailing, green subway tiles, bold botanical wallpaper, and eclectic mix of vintage furniture and crockery.

The design for this window display was informed by the Cake Room's unique style and personality, which enables the display to look absolutely "at home" in the store.

I created one super-sized flower to provide a focal point for the display. The copper pearlescent paper bounces light to catch the eyes of passersby, and I used the same paper for the standard-sized flowers in the backdrop. Using the same color for the petals and center details gives a streamlined aesthetic. I also used copper-colored gourd pins and floristry wire to add continuity and attention to detail.

The smaller flowers are on green cards that graduate from a dark green at the top to a white at the bottom of each drop. These drops complement the oversized flower, framing and filling space while not blocking the light.

1.   The first step for this project was to show Lauren, the owner, my idea in sketch form.

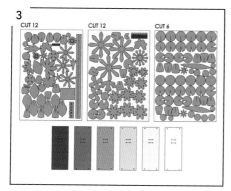

4a

4d

4b

4e

4c

4f

2. I then measured the space and moved on to scaled drawings to work out the exact sizes of the props and layout of the backdrop.

3. The next step was to set up the files that needed to be sent to my digital cutting machine, and cut out the 1,500+ components for the display.

4a–f. Then, it was time to start production.

5a

5e

5b

5f

5c

5d

5g

5a–g. The finished small flowers

6a–d. I prelinked all of the flower cards, in order. This was to make the installation as quick and easy as possible.

The Cake Room has a preexisting copper rail at the back of their windows that is used for art exhibitions, so I used that to hang the drops.

6a

6c

6b

6d

FLORAL CLOUD

I have always admired fresh floristry work, and hanging installations have increased in popularity over the last few years. I wanted to create my own paper floral cloud. It could be used in a retail display, in a domestic interior, at a wedding, or at any other special event. I have styled it as though it were above a sweetheart table at a wedding. Having a hanging display adds interest to an event space, and in this set up it also leaves more space on the table for place settings and other décor.

I chose an autumnal pallette, adding in pops of yellow, coral, and bright pink to lift it. Although the color palette isn't as realistic as, for example, the Bouquet, I have deliberatly kept all foliage in very neutral colors and the flowers in the punchier tones to mimic something more natural.

This installation uses over sixty flowers and around thirty different foliage stems and large leaves. I used a range of different paper textures and finishes to give an eclectic, final aesthetic. The flowers and leaves are attached to four metal wreath frames, which I joined to each other at varying angles. This allowed me to feed the stems into the cloud and bend/wrap them around the frames and each other.

I wanted an asymmetric shape to the piece and sketched the idea out before I began. I approached the arrangement in much the same way as the Table Arrangement: starting by setting the overall shape with foliage before layering in the flowers. The hanging drops are made up of Base Cones that have been threaded onto transparent nylon wire and held in place with crimp beads as used in jewelry making.

WEDDING ARCH

This 6.5 ft. (2 m) tall, bespoke, plywood arch features over-sized paper flowers and leaves that were inspired by 1940–1960s textile, furniture, and interior design. The stylized leaves mimic the geometric patterns of the period, and the large sunray petals are reminiscent of iconic '50s and '60s mirrors and clocks.

I designed and made the arch itself so that it could be taken apart and stored easily. This means that different designs can be applied to the structure. I planned the back drop out, to scale, so that I could get the flowers to the correct proportions. The final result is pretty close to the drawing, which is always pleasing!

TECHNIQUES TO STUDY

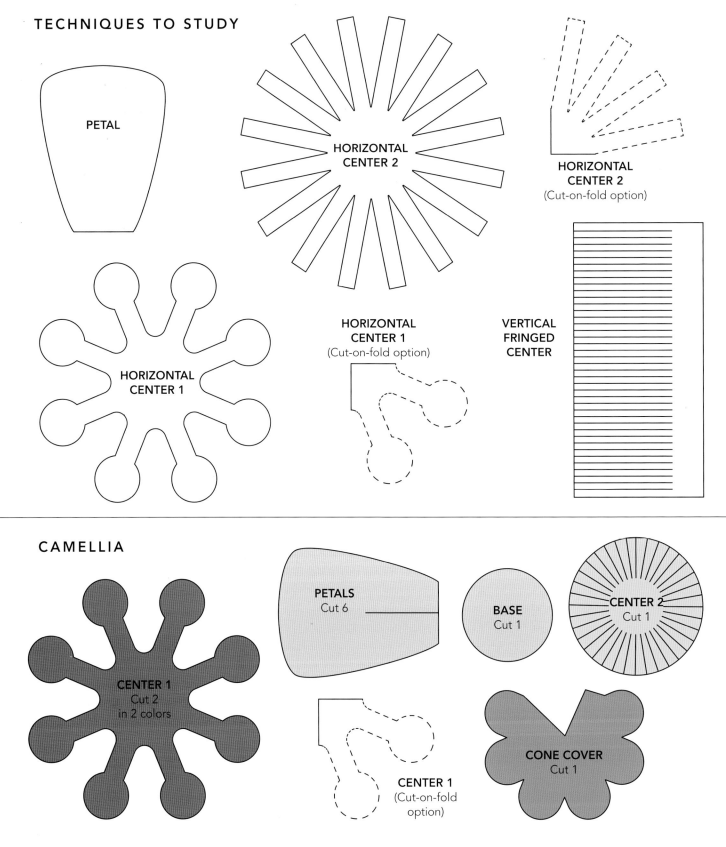

PETAL

HORIZONTAL
CENTER 2

HORIZONTAL
CENTER 2
(Cut-on-fold option)

HORIZONTAL
CENTER 1

HORIZONTAL
CENTER 1
(Cut-on-fold option)

VERTICAL
FRINGED
CENTER

CAMELLIA

CENTER 1
Cut 2
in 2 colors

PETALS
Cut 6

BASE
Cut 1

CENTER 2
Cut 1

CENTER 1
(Cut-on-fold
option)

CONE COVER
Cut 1

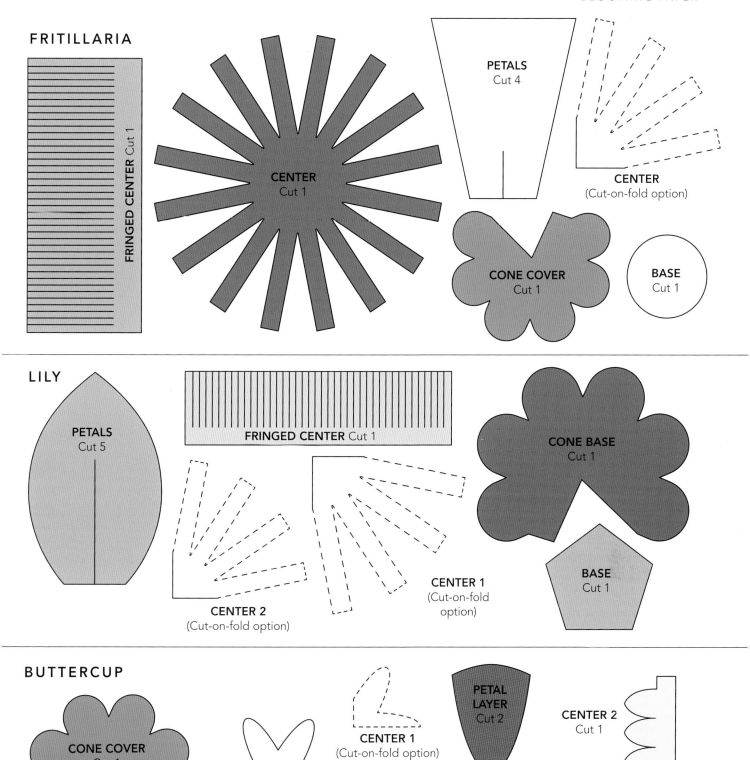

FRITILLARIA

FRINGED CENTER Cut 1

CENTER
Cut 1

PETALS
Cut 4

CENTER
(Cut-on-fold option)

CONE COVER
Cut 1

BASE
Cut 1

LILY

PETALS
Cut 5

FRINGED CENTER Cut 1

CONE BASE
Cut 1

CENTER 2
(Cut-on-fold option)

CENTER 1
(Cut-on-fold
option)

BASE
Cut 1

BUTTERCUP

CONE COVER
Cut 1

CENTER 1
Cut 1

CENTER 1
(Cut-on-fold option)

PETAL
LAYER
Cut 2

CENTER 2
Cut 1

147

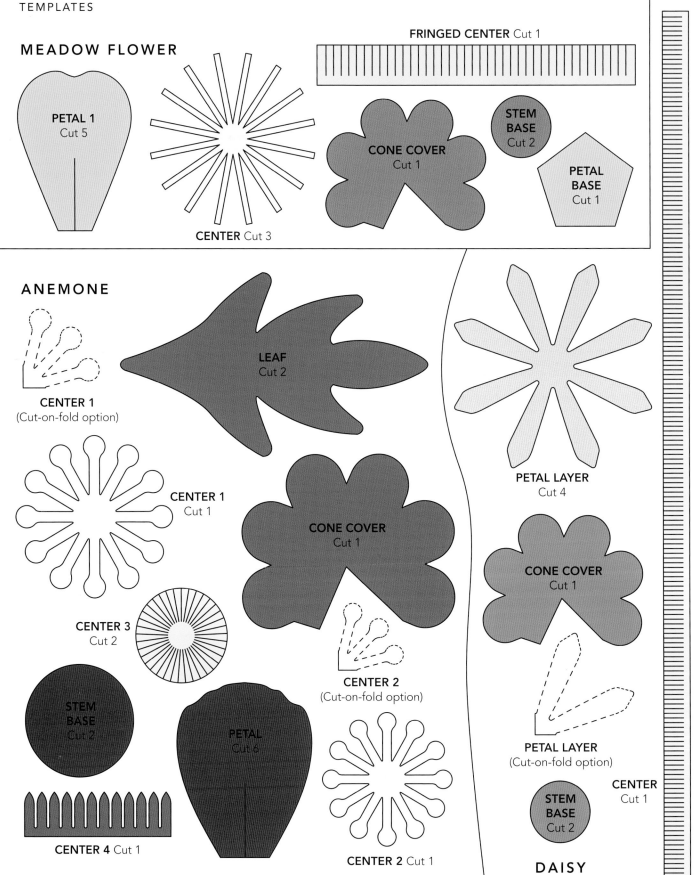

MEADOW FLOWER

PETAL 1
Cut 5

CENTER Cut 3

FRINGED CENTER Cut 1

CONE COVER
Cut 1

STEM
BASE
Cut 2

PETAL
BASE
Cut 1

ANEMONE

CENTER 1
(Cut-on-fold option)

CENTER 1
Cut 1

CENTER 3
Cut 2

STEM
BASE
Cut 2

CENTER 4 Cut 1

PETAL
Cut 6

LEAF
Cut 2

CONE COVER
Cut 1

CENTER 2
(Cut-on-fold option)

CENTER 2 Cut 1

PETAL LAYER
Cut 4

CONE COVER
Cut 1

PETAL LAYER
(Cut-on-fold option)

STEM
BASE
Cut 2

CENTER
Cut 1

DAISY

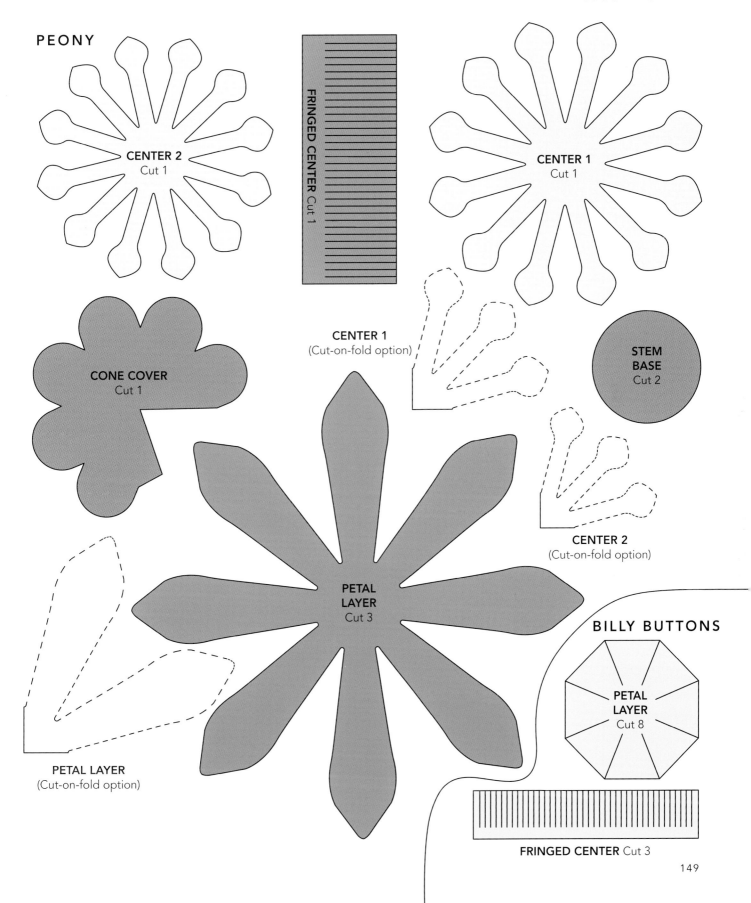

PEONY

CENTER 2
Cut 1

FRINGED CENTER Cut 1

CENTER 1
Cut 1

CONE COVER
Cut 1

CENTER 1
(Cut-on-fold option)

STEM
BASE
Cut 2

PETAL
LAYER
Cut 3

CENTER 2
(Cut-on-fold option)

BILLY BUTTONS

PETAL
LAYER
Cut 8

PETAL LAYER
(Cut-on-fold option)

FRINGED CENTER Cut 3

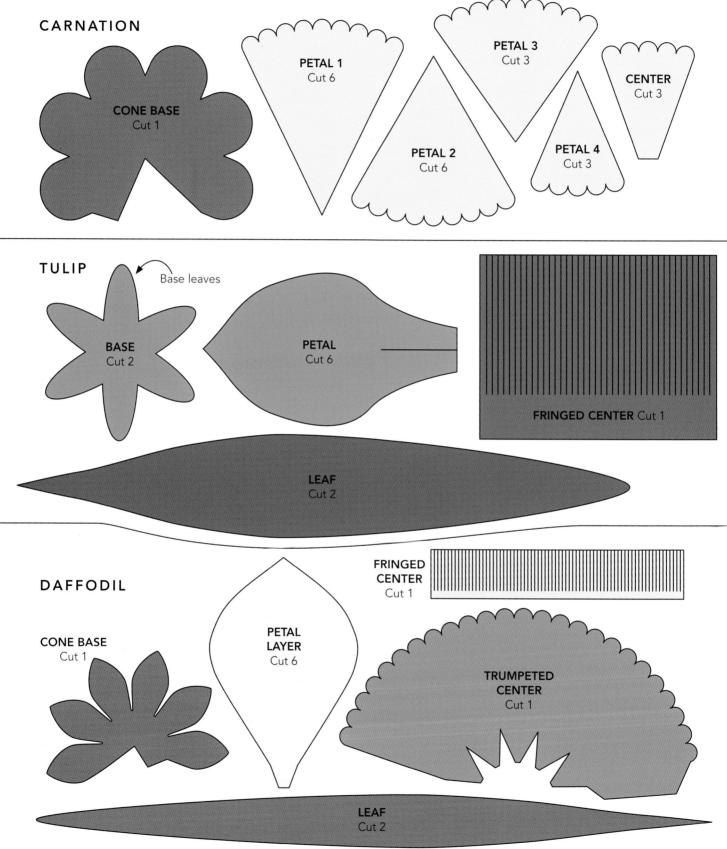

CARNATION

CONE BASE
Cut 1

PETAL 1
Cut 6

PETAL 2
Cut 6

PETAL 3
Cut 3

PETAL 4
Cut 3

CENTER
Cut 3

TULIP

Base leaves

BASE
Cut 2

PETAL
Cut 6

FRINGED CENTER Cut 1

LEAF
Cut 2

DAFFODIL

FRINGED
CENTER
Cut 1

CONE BASE
Cut 1

PETAL
LAYER
Cut 6

TRUMPETED
CENTER
Cut 1

LEAF
Cut 2

DAHLIA

PETAL LAYER 1
Cut 3

PETAL LAYER 2
Cut 3

PETAL LAYER 3
Cut 2

CENTER Cut 1

STEM BASE
Cut 2

PETAL LAYER 6
Cut 1

PETAL LAYER 5
Cut 1

PETAL LAYER 4
Cut 1

INNER PETALS
Cut 1

CONE COVER
Cut 1

PETAL LAYERS 4-6
(Cut-on-fold option)

LEAF
Cut 2

PETAL LAYER 2
(Cut on-fold-option)

PETAL LAYER 3
(Cut-on-fold option)

PETAL LAYER 1
(Cut-on-fold option)

INNER PETALS
(Cut-on-fold option)

PEONY BUD

BASE
Cut 1

PETAL LAYER
Cut 1

PETAL LAYER
(Cut-on-fold option)

BASE
(Cut-on-fold option)

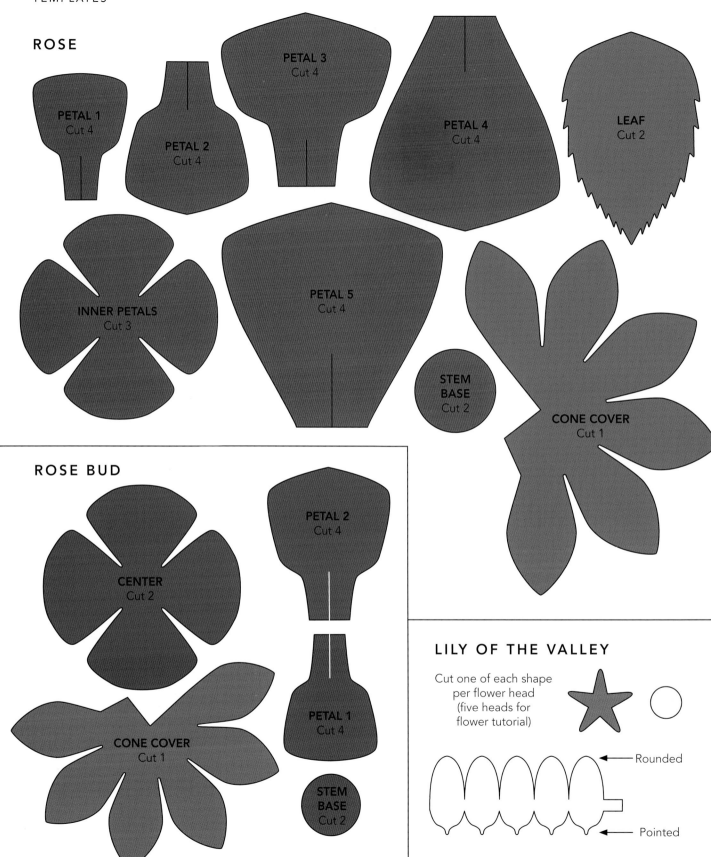

ROSE

PETAL 1
Cut 4

PETAL 2
Cut 4

PETAL 3
Cut 4

PETAL 4
Cut 4

LEAF
Cut 2

INNER PETALS
Cut 3

PETAL 5
Cut 4

STEM BASE
Cut 2

CONE COVER
Cut 1

ROSE BUD

CENTER
Cut 2

PETAL 2
Cut 4

CONE COVER
Cut 1

PETAL 1
Cut 4

STEM BASE
Cut 2

LILY OF THE VALLEY

Cut one of each shape
per flower head
(five heads for
flower tutorial)

← Rounded

← Pointed

RANUNCULUS

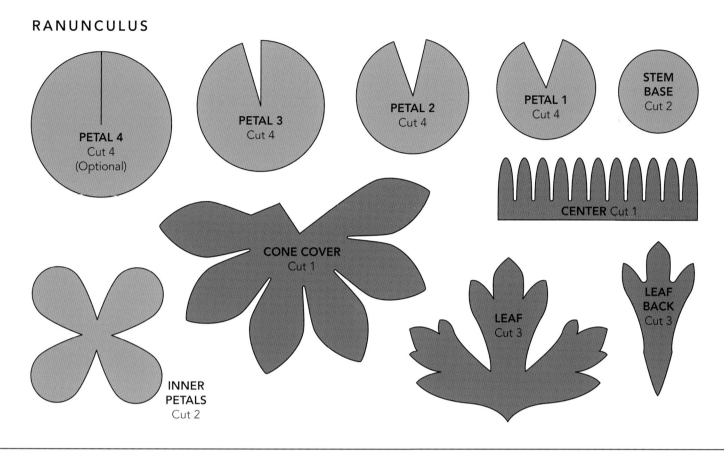

PETAL 4
Cut 4
(Optional)

PETAL 3
Cut 4

PETAL 2
Cut 4

PETAL 1
Cut 4

STEM BASE
Cut 2

CENTER Cut 1

CONE COVER
Cut 1

INNER PETALS
Cut 2

LEAF
Cut 3

LEAF BACK
Cut 3

FREESIA

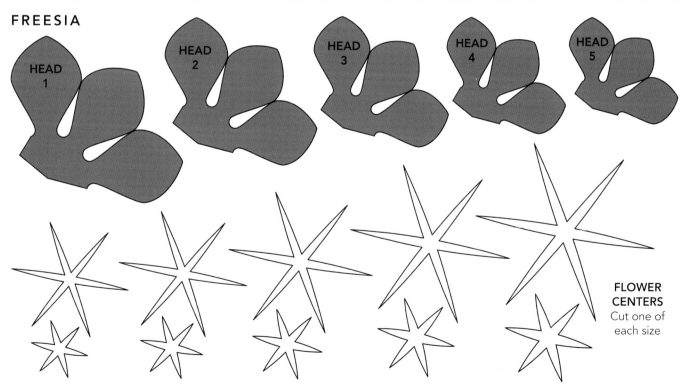

HEAD 1

HEAD 2

HEAD 3

HEAD 4

HEAD 5

FLOWER CENTERS
Cut one of each size

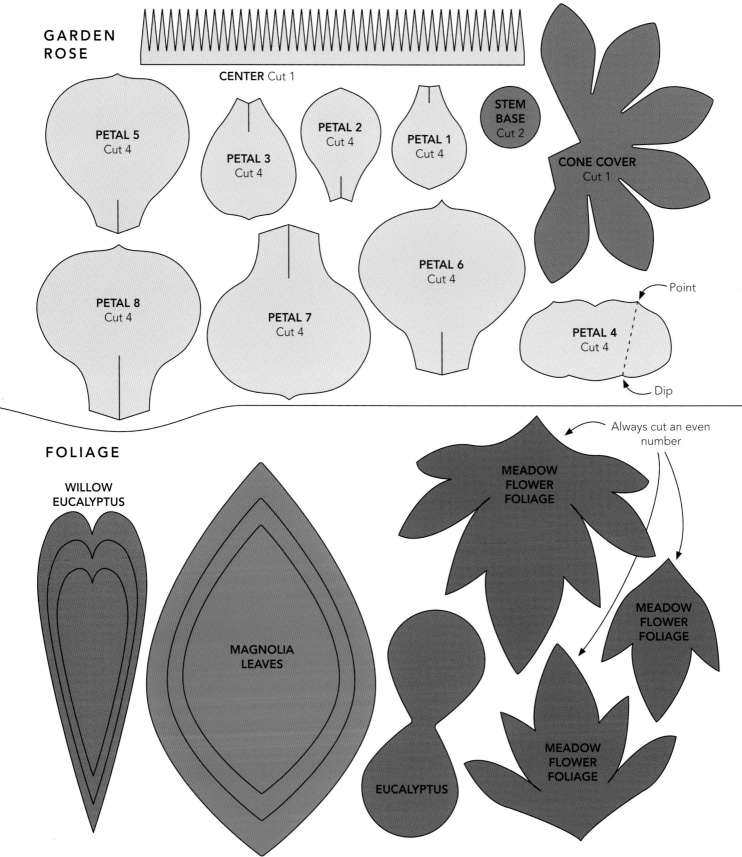

GARDEN ROSE

CENTER Cut 1

PETAL 5
Cut 4

PETAL 3
Cut 4

PETAL 2
Cut 4

PETAL 1
Cut 4

STEM BASE
Cut 2

CONE COVER
Cut 1

PETAL 8
Cut 4

PETAL 7
Cut 4

PETAL 6
Cut 4

Point

PETAL 4
Cut 4

Dip

FOLIAGE

WILLOW
EUCALYPTUS

MAGNOLIA
LEAVES

Always cut an even
number

MEADOW
FLOWER
FOLIAGE

MEADOW
FLOWER
FOLIAGE

EUCALYPTUS

MEADOW
FLOWER
FOLIAGE

ALTERNATIVE PETAL SHAPES

Use these to design your own flowers

ALTERNATIVE COMPONENT SHAPES

Use these to design your own flowers

BASES AND CONE COVERS

Use these to design your own flowers

SEVEN-PETAL BASE

FIVE-PETAL BASE

EIGHT-PETAL BASE

SIX-PETAL BASE

CAKE TOPPER
Alternative numbers

Cut 1

MINI DAISIES
Cut 8

SMALL
BUTTER
CUP
Cut 2

CENTER
Cut 1

Cut 1

(Dashed line shows
on fold option)

CENTER 2 Cut 1

Cut 1

Cut 1

ALSO CUT
1 Meadow Flower
1 standard Buttercup

BUTTONHOLE
IAN

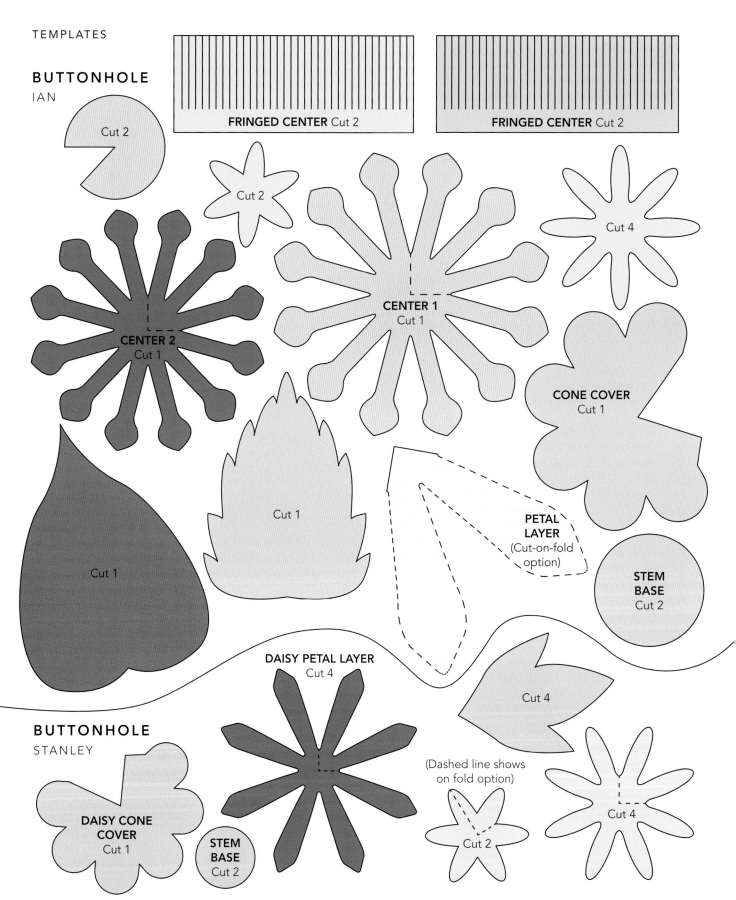

FRINGED CENTER Cut 2

FRINGED CENTER Cut 2

Cut 2

Cut 2

Cut 4

CENTER 2
Cut 1

CENTER 1
Cut 1

CONE COVER
Cut 1

Cut 1

Cut 1

PETAL
LAYER
(Cut-on-fold
option)

STEM
BASE
Cut 2

DAISY PETAL LAYER
Cut 4

Cut 4

BUTTONHOLE
STANLEY

(Dashed line shows
on fold option)

DAISY CONE
COVER
Cut 1

STEM
BASE
Cut 2

Cut 2

Cut 4

DAISY CENTER Cut 1

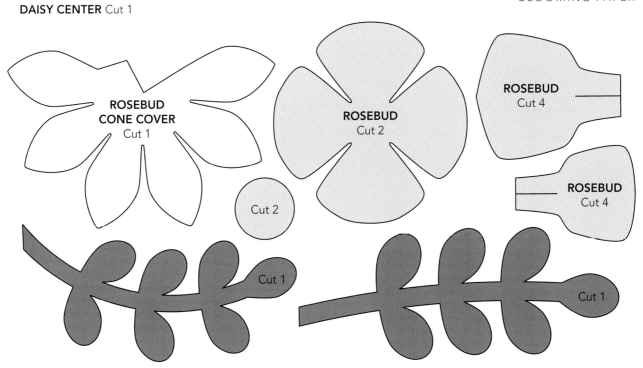

ROSEBUD CONE COVER
Cut 1

Cut 2

ROSEBUD
Cut 2

ROSEBUD
Cut 4

ROSEBUD
Cut 4

Cut 1

Cut 1

BUTTONHOLE

MIKE

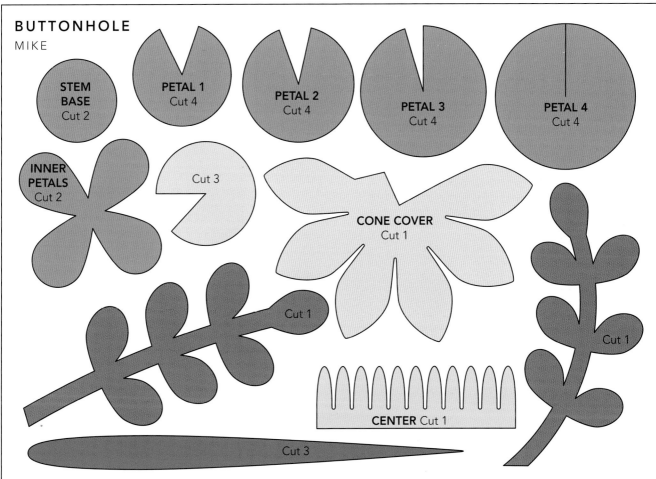

STEM BASE
Cut 2

PETAL 1
Cut 4

PETAL 2
Cut 4

PETAL 3
Cut 4

PETAL 4
Cut 4

INNER PETALS
Cut 2

Cut 3

CONE COVER
Cut 1

Cut 1

Cut 1

CENTER Cut 1

Cut 3

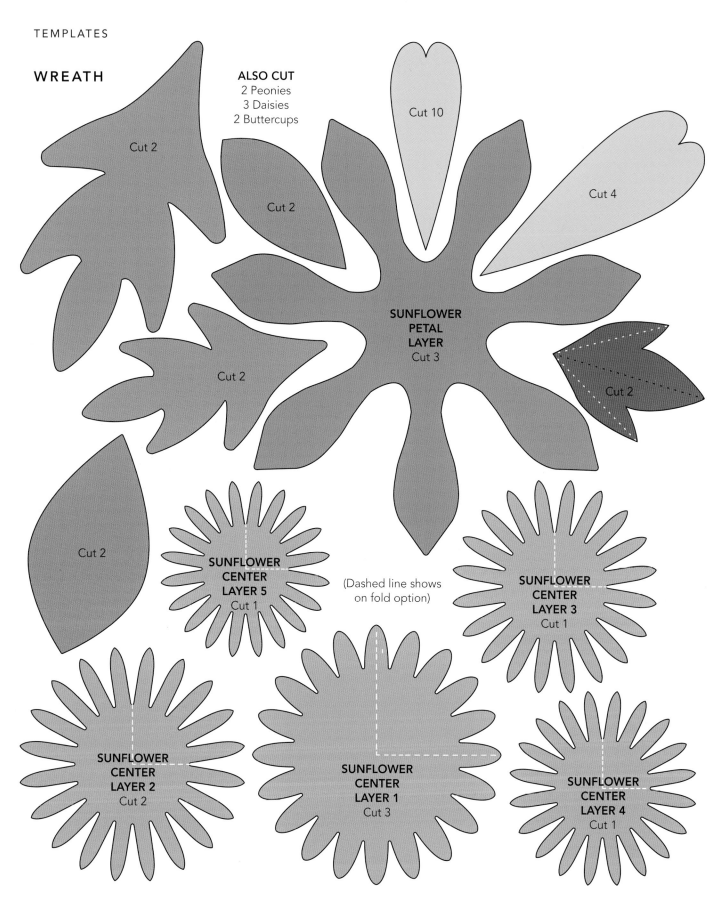

WREATH

ALSO CUT
2 Peonies
3 Daisies
2 Buttercups

Cut 2

Cut 2

Cut 10

Cut 4

Cut 2

SUNFLOWER
PETAL
LAYER
Cut 3

Cut 2

Cut 2

SUNFLOWER
CENTER
LAYER 5
Cut 1

(Dashed line shows
on fold option)

SUNFLOWER
CENTER
LAYER 3
Cut 1

SUNFLOWER
CENTER
LAYER 2
Cut 2

SUNFLOWER
CENTER
LAYER 1
Cut 3

SUNFLOWER
CENTER
LAYER 4
Cut 1

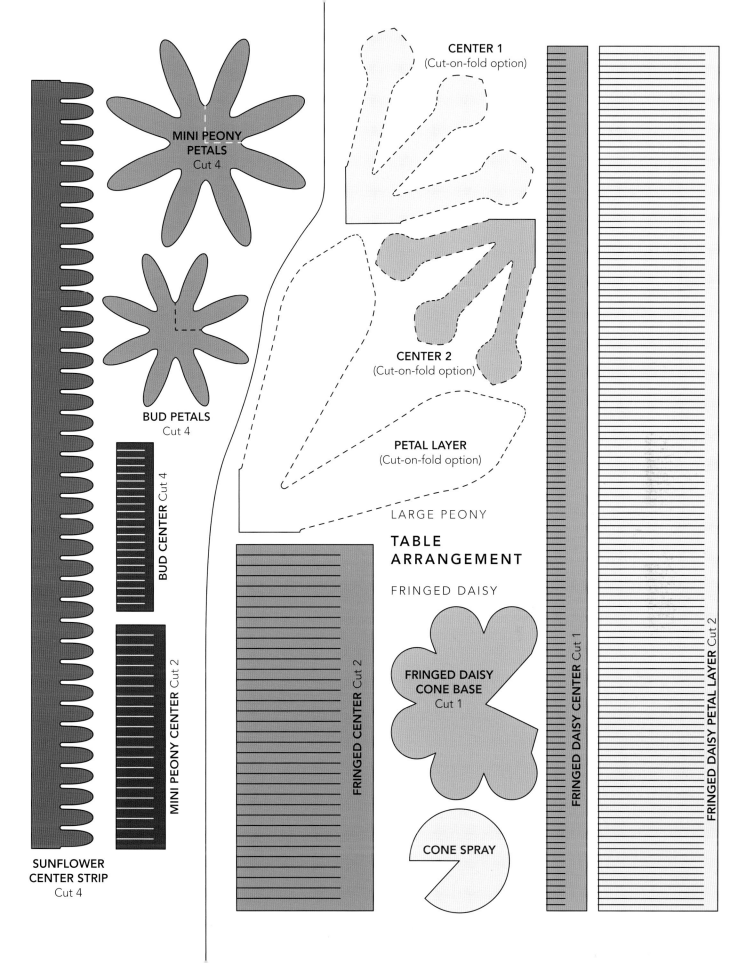

MINI PEONY
PETALS
Cut 4

BUD PETALS
Cut 4

BUD CENTER Cut 4

MINI PEONY CENTER Cut 2

SUNFLOWER
CENTER STRIP
Cut 4

CENTER 1
(Cut-on-fold option)

CENTER 2
(Cut-on-fold option)

PETAL LAYER
(Cut-on-fold option)

LARGE PEONY

TABLE
ARRANGEMENT

FRINGED DAISY

FRINGED CENTER Cut 2

FRINGED DAISY
CONE BASE
Cut 1

CONE SPRAY

FRINGED DAISY CENTER Cut 1

FRINGED DAISY PETAL LAYER Cut 2

CHANDELIER

PEONIES

ALSO CUT
1 standard Peony
(Dashed line shows
on fold option)

SMALL PEONY
Cut 3

MEDIUM PEONY
Cut 3

SMALL CENTER 2 Cut 1

**MEDIUM CENTER 2
/ SMALL CENTER 1**
Cut 2

MEDIUM CENTER 1
Cut 1

SMALL FRINGED CENTER Cut 2

MEDIUM CENTER 2 Cut 1

MEDIUM FRINGED CENTER Cut 2

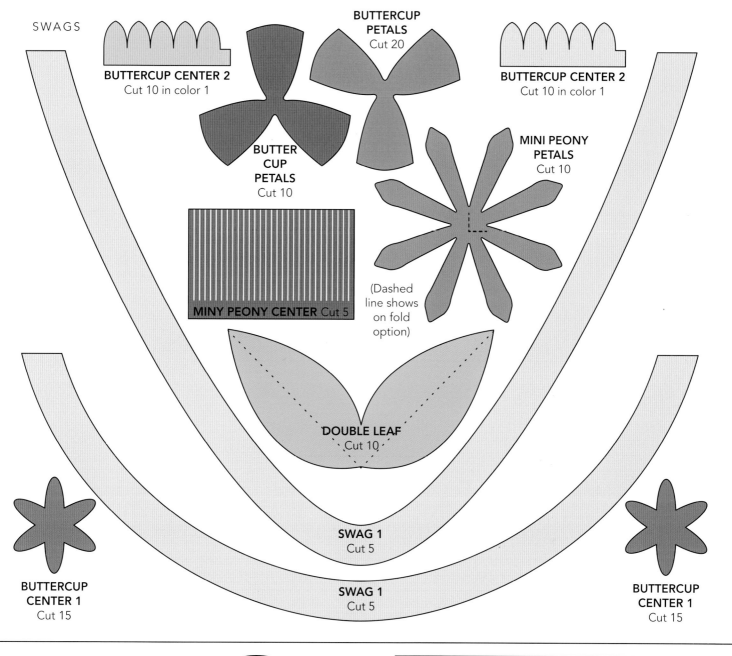

SWAGS

BUTTERCUP CENTER 2
Cut 10 in color 1

BUTTERCUP
PETALS
Cut 20

BUTTERCUP CENTER 2
Cut 10 in color 1

BUTTER
CUP
PETALS
Cut 10

MINI PEONY
PETALS
Cut 10

MINY PEONY CENTER Cut 5

(Dashed
line shows
on fold
option)

DOUBLE LEAF
Cut 10

SWAG 1
Cut 5

SWAG 1
Cut 5

BUTTERCUP
CENTER 1
Cut 15

BUTTERCUP
CENTER 1
Cut 15

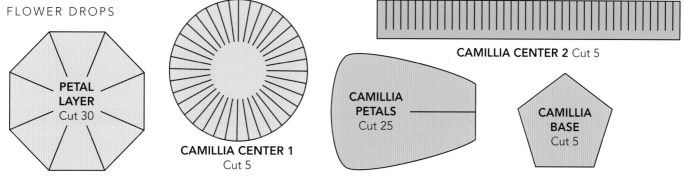

FLOWER DROPS

PETAL
LAYER
Cut 30

CAMILLIA CENTER 1
Cut 5

CAMILLIA CENTER 2 Cut 5

CAMILLIA
PETALS
Cut 25

CAMILLIA
BASE
Cut 5

TEMPLATES

FLOWER DROPS
CONTINUED

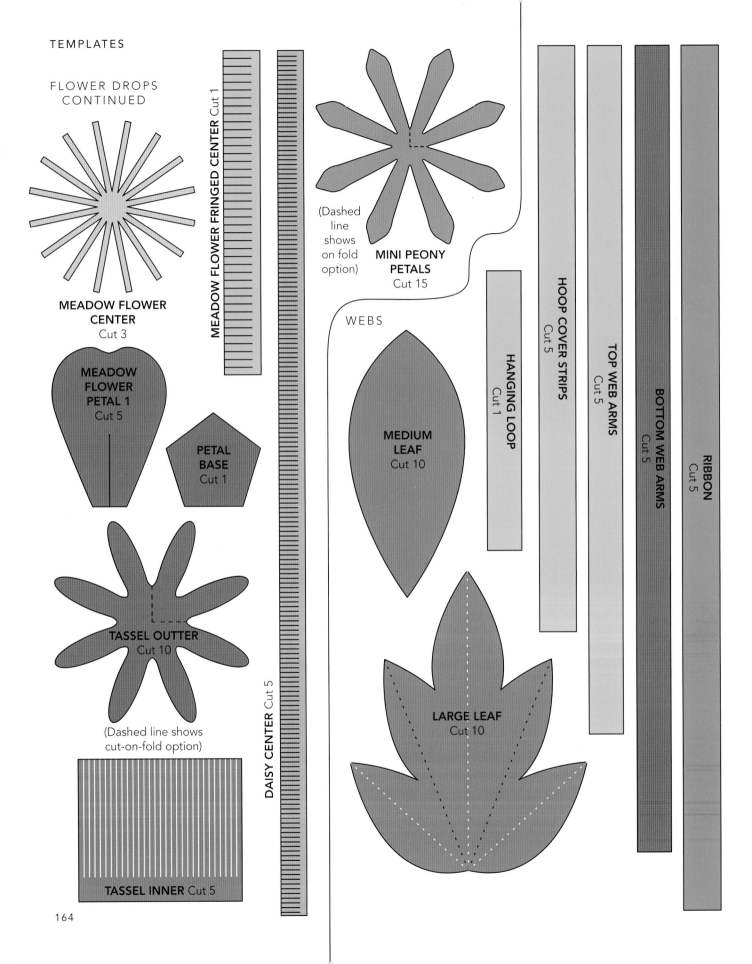

MEADOW FLOWER
CENTER
Cut 3

MEADOW FLOWER FRINGED CENTER Cut 1

MEADOW
FLOWER
PETAL 1
Cut 5

PETAL
BASE
Cut 1

TASSEL OUTTER
Cut 10

(Dashed line shows
cut-on-fold option)

TASSEL INNER Cut 5

DAISY CENTER Cut 5

(Dashed
line
shows
on fold
option)

MINI PEONY
PETALS
Cut 15

WEBS

MEDIUM
LEAF
Cut 10

LARGE LEAF
Cut 10

HANGING LOOP
Cut 1

HOOP COVER STRIPS
Cut 5

TOP WEB ARMS
Cut 5

BOTTOM WEB ARMS
Cut 5

RIBBON
Cut 5

164

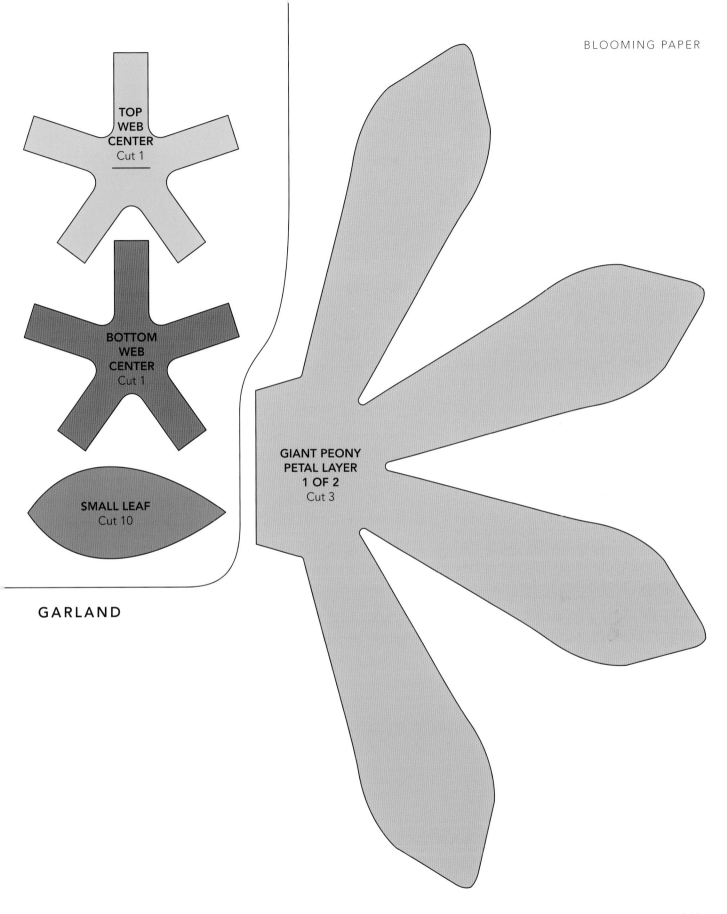

**TOP
WEB
CENTER**
Cut 1

**BOTTOM
WEB
CENTER**
Cut 1

SMALL LEAF
Cut 10

**GIANT PEONY
PETAL LAYER
1 OF 2**
Cut 3

GARLAND

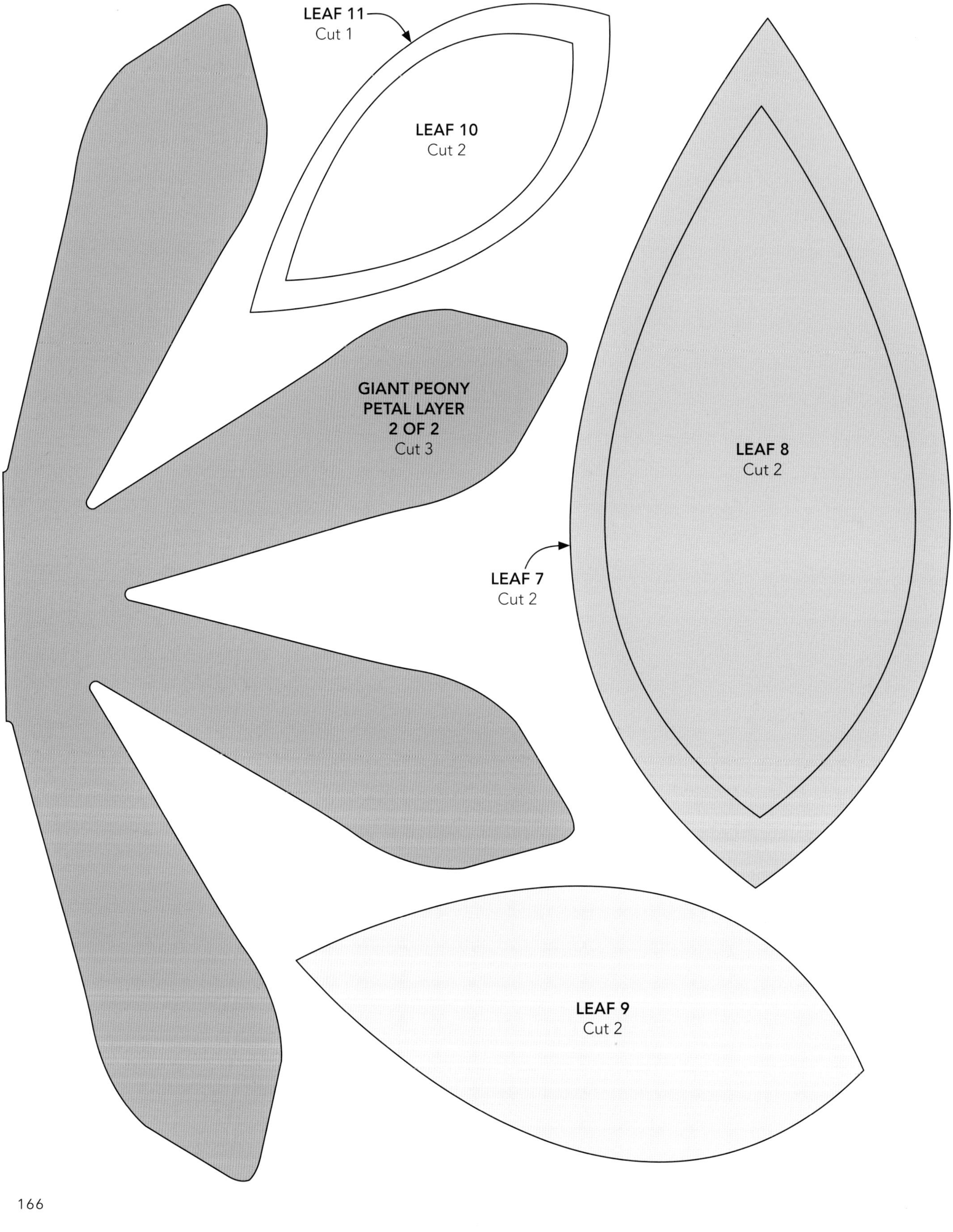

LEAF 11
Cut 1

LEAF 10
Cut 2

LEAF 8
Cut 2

**GIANT PEONY
PETAL LAYER
2 OF 2**
Cut 3

LEAF 7
Cut 2

LEAF 9
Cut 2

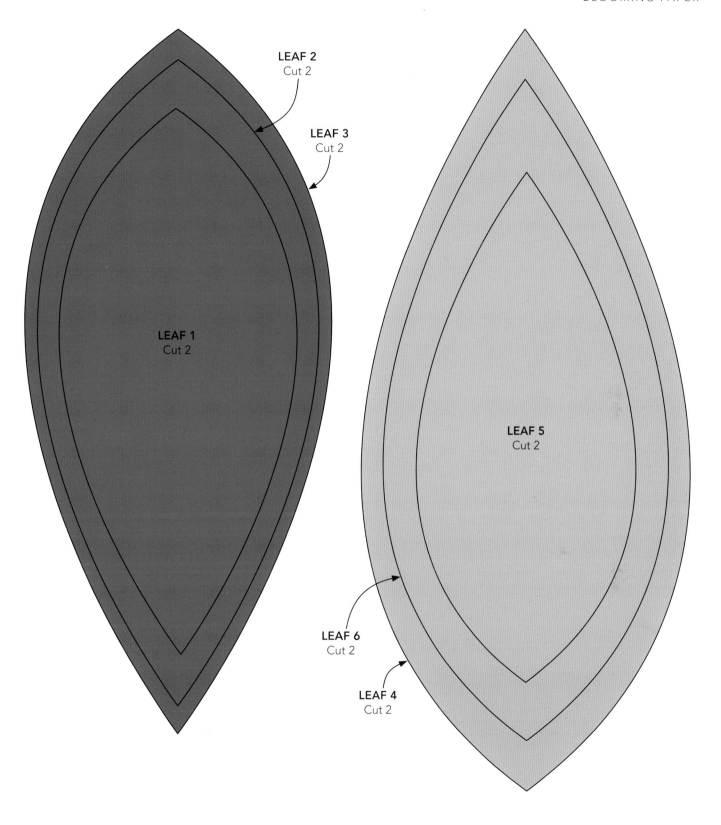

LEAF 2
Cut 2

LEAF 3
Cut 2

LEAF 1
Cut 2

LEAF 5
Cut 2

LEAF 6
Cut 2

LEAF 4
Cut 2

Laura Reed is an award-winning, professional designer and maker. Her work has been featured in magazines, books, and online media. She has also appeared on television and won the competition she was competing in. Laura studied furniture and product design at university and has a career background in retail display design.

Laura started her own company in 2012, following her own wedding. Among many other things, she made a lot of paper items for her wedding, especially paper flowers. This got her noticed, and, as time went on, she became known for her paper flowers. Laura is self-taught, and over the years, she has honed her skills and her designs have become more elaborate.

Laura has now worked with hundreds of couples, making a range of pieces from buttonholes and bouquets to backdrops and large-scale installations. She has also worked with brands and retailers on window displays and props for photo shoots and editorial imagery.

In 2016, Laura started to teach paper flower workshops. She designed the course structure and the reusable template kits that she teaches with. These kits are currently in production and will be available to buy soon.